Creation Versus Evolution
A Biblical and Scientific Study

Rockie Sue Fordham

©copyright 2009 Rockie Sue Fordham. All rights reserved.

First published by RockLan Publications 09/3/2009

Preface

Based on current research, at least 70% of teenagers raised in church claim they will walk away as soon as possible. Why? Why are we losing so many of our youth? I believe the answer lies in our society teaching evolution as scientific fact. From the time our children are very young they hear this theory being pushed through animal documentaries, movies, and even cartoons. Our media has utterly engulfed our culture in this worldly teaching. That's why we, as parents and teachers of the truth, must give them the necessary ammunition to counter this philosophy, not only so they can witness it to their friends but so they can stand firm in their own faith.

How does the world try to indoctrinate our youth? It teaches them that evolution is science not religion, that it has been proven by scientific finds such as fossils and dating methods, and that only "ignorant and unlearned" people still believe in a God who created. At the same time, our youth have studied in Genesis 1 that God spoke the entire universe into existence in merely six days. They are taught that one is science, but the other must be accepted by faith alone.

But is evolution true science? Before answering that we must understand that there are two types of science; operational and historical. Operational science must be observable with one or more of our five senses or experimentally repeatable so that it can be tested and potentially falsifiable. Historical science is very different. It involves interpreting evidence from the past, and when you recognize that everyone has presupposed philosophical ideas that bias their interpretations, it helps you to understand that historical science is not on the same playing field as operational science. In other words, neither creation nor evolution fit into the observable science category; therefore they are both historical science and include speculation, personal bias, assumptions and evidence collected.

Now let's return to my original question, "Why are we losing so many of our youth?" Evolutionists ignore these definitions of science and deceptively teach our youth that evolution is true "operational" science and the creation story merely religion, and by doing so they successfully entangle Satan's lies with scientific truth. It is no wonder that so many of our youth, who are certainly intelligent enough to realize the biblical creation story and evolution don't mix, end up leaving the church forever. After all, if the very first five words of the Bible, "In the beginning God created . . ." aren't true, why should they trust its message of salvation?

In the following material you will evaluate and contrast the biblical story of creation with Darwin's theory of evolution. You will examine what the Bible actually teaches, the scientific evidence in support of the biblical creation story, and in what ways operational science is consistent with the Bible and inconsistent with the theory of evolution. I have also included some suggested readings that correlate with each chapter from Lee Strobel's book, *The Case for a Creator* and Tom DeRosa's book, *Evolution's Fatal Fruit*. In *The Case for a Creator* Lee Strobel interviews several elite scientists, each working in a different field of science, to gather their insight into why they—as scientists—believe in a God who created the universe. Tom DeRosa's book, *Evolution's Fatal Fruit*, gives credence to the atrocities dealt upon mankind because of Darwin's godless theory.

Course Objective and Information for Christian School Teachers Desiring 5 Biblical CEU's

Creation Versus Evolution: A Biblical and Scientific Study is designed to evaluate and contrast the biblical story of creation with Darwin's theory of evolution. As previously stated, this course examines what the Bible actually teaches, the scientific evidence in support of the biblical creation story, and in what ways operational science is consistent with the Bible and inconsistent with the theory of evolution.

If you are taking this course for the purpose of receiving 5 biblical CEU's, you will also need to complete all included worksheets and suggested reading assignments. The course will tell you when there is a worksheet or additional required reading to be completed—directions are in red ink if you're using the Kindle e-book version. Please feel free to contact me with any comments or observations through www.rocklanpublications.com. I would love to hear from you frequently. When you have completed the course, workbook (found at the back of the material) and videos included, send your 5 page paper (detailed in the workbook) with the Completion Form (found at the back of the workbook) and $80.00 to the following address to receive your CEU's. (Rockie Fordham, P.O. Box 595, Fountain, CO 80817) As you work this course you will be required to read Lee Strobel's book, *The Case for a Creator* and Tom DeRosa's book, *Evolution's Fatal Fruit* and to view your choice of at least six hours chosen from the following videos. (These are excellent videos to request your Librarian to purchase for your school library. Additional creation videos may be substituted in their place if you cannot get access to them, but they must be videos presented by creation believing scientists.)

Required: Check out a copy of the 1960 version of *Inherit the Wind* (1999 is alright if necessary).

Additional Videos:

Expelled: No Intelligence Allowed, Ben Stein, Vivendi Entertainment, Premise Media Corporation, 2008

Ultimate Apologetics by Dr. Jason Lisle

(This is a package of four videos titled *The Ultimate Proof of Creation, Evolution and Logical Falicies, Neclear Strength Apologetics Pt. 1* & *Nuclear Strength Apologetics Pt. 2*)

Noah's Ark on Ararat: Encounters with the Unexplained, Grissly Adams Production, Inc., Baker

The Case for a Creator by Lee Strobel

The Case for Christ by Lee Strobel

Chapter 1: The Re-Writing of History

Suggested Reading: Chapter 1 in *The Case for a Creator* (It is my suggestion that you read with a highlighter in hand, marking the references which are most significant to you for future use.)

Ignorant and Unlearned Christians?

My son, Daniel, who was attending his first year of college, came home one day and said, "Mom, you're not going to believe what my professor said today." Curious, I asked, "What?" Daniel answered, "He said, 'Only ignorant and unlearned Christians still believe in a God who created.'" That statement should have been surprising to me, after all, America was founded as a Christian nation with Christian principles. Yet it was no surprise at all. Actually, this professor's statement is typical of the kind of indoctrination that many so-call "opened-minded and educated people" are forcing upon our society today. But how truthful is this statement? Do "only ignorant and unlearned" individuals still believe in a God who created? Let's examine a few of these so-called *ignorant and unlearned Christians*.

First, in an article titled, *Cosmology in crisis—a conference report,* 30 concerned scientists published an open letter to the global scientific community in *New Scientist* in which they protested the stranglehold of the Big Bang theory on cosmological research and funding (John Hartnett).

Second, Lee Strobel tells of a time in his book *The Case for Christ* when he was honored to be the moderator of a debate between William Lane Craig, Ph.D., D.Th., and an atheist selected by the national spokesman for American Atheists, Inc. In this debate Dr. Craig defended Christianity before a crowd of nearly 8,000, with countless others listening on more than one hundred radio stations across the country. Lee Strobel writes, "As moderator . . . I marveled as Craig politely but powerfully built the case for Christianity while simultaneously dismantling the arguments for atheism. From where I was sitting, I could watch the faces of people as they discovered—many for the first time—that Christianity can stand up to rational analysis and rugged scrutiny. In the end it was no contest. Among those who had entered the auditorium that evening as avowed atheists, agnostics, or skeptics, an overwhelming 82 percent walked out concluding that the case for Christianity had been the most compelling. Forty-seven people entered as nonbelievers and exited as Christians—Craig's arguments for the faith were that persuasive, especially compared with the paucity of evidence for atheism. Incidentally, nobody became an atheist" (Strobel 277).

Third, in *Creation* magazine, June—August 2004, there was an article titled *An Awesome Mind.* This article goes on to examine one of Christianity's foremost defenders, Jonathan Sarfati. This *ignorant and unlearned Christian* "obtained a B.Sc. (Hons.) in Chemistry with two physics papers submitted (nuclear and condensed matter physics). His Ph. D. in Chemistry was awarded for a thesis entitled 'A Spectroscopic Study of Some Chalcogenide Ring and Cage Molecules'. He has co-authored papers in mainstream scientific journals on high-temperature superconductors and selenium-containing ring and cage-shaped molecules." His books *Refuting Evolution* and *Refuting Evolution 2* have become best-sellers—standard reading for Christians who wish to be able to defend their faith. He and some friends co-founded the Wellington Christian Apologetics Society (www.christianapologetics.org).

What led Jonathan to become a Christian? It was logical reasoning, not emotion or a life crisis. Jonathan not only has a very logical mind, he also has an amazing memory for details. "A former New Zealand Chess Champion, he represented New Zealand in three Chess Olympiads, and he has drawn a tournament game with former world champion Boris Spassky. The International Chess Federation awarded him the title F.I.D.E. Master in 1988."

While speaking at Answers in Genesis conferences and camps, Jonathan has become famous for accepting challenges against multiple chess players simultaneously, while blind-folded, against seeing opponents. The moves his opponents make are merely called out to him. At one challenge presented in Sydney, Australia, he competed against 12 opponents (blind-folded and with his back turned away from the boards) all at the same time. The following day when a scientist recalled a specific move from one of his opponents, Jonathan quickly corrected the man saying he was mistaken concerning which board had made that move. Link to the following site for the complete story: http://creation.com/an-awesome-mind-creation-magazine-jonathan-sarfatiinterview, or do an online search of 'jonathan sarfati an awesome mind' and click on the site.

Science: A Christian Heritage

Many secular scientists promote the propaganda that a materialistic belief—a belief that excludes God and his work in creation—is necessary for the practice of true science by claiming Christianity and modern science are incompatible. Some go so far as to claim a belief in God is even detrimental to the practice of real science; that they actually war against each other. Yet the hard facts of history teach the exact opposite. So the questions to ask are, "Is the rewriting of history really that dangerous?" and "Does it really matter where modern science originated?" My answer is yes. Why? Because the rewriting of history is not only used as a crucial tool to sway students away from pride in their country, it is also used to sway them away from belief in their Creator.

Historically, the roots of modern science were cultivated in Christian Europe—a regional setting that was entrenched in the Christian worldview—and among Christian scientists, many of whom were very interested in theology and outspoken defenders of their faith. In fact, at least two-thirds of the founding members of the Royal Society of England (1660)—England's premier scientific organization whose purpose was to share and further scientific studies, were Puritans. Among these Puritans and early European believers were the discoverers of the laws of gravity, motion, thermodynamics, chemistry, heredity, and biogenesis.

Furthermore, in an era when the "eternal universe concept" was accepted as scientific fact, these believers stood alone in their rejection of this theory, and their rejection was based solely upon their belief in the authority of God's Word and the biblical story of creation. Some secular writers have conceded this point, acknowledging that only within the framework of the Christian worldview did the necessary makeup exist to generate true modern science (Bumbulis). If, as argued by many unbelievers, modern science and belief in God are incompatible, why is the very heritage of true science inseparable from Christianity?

What is modern science? It is man's attempt to discover the workings of nature, and although the practice of science isn't specifically about technology, technological discoveries are its natural result. After all, our advanced technical lifestyle didn't magically appear in the 21st century, it slowly evolved over the past millennium as European scientists, believing that the rational God of the Bible would create a rational universe, set out to discover the inner workings of God's creation. Thus, modern science was born.

The following men are some of these pioneers of modern science, and their belief in a Creator is what motivated them to search for the truth of natural laws even before the existence of such laws were known?

John Ambrose Fleming, inventor of the Fleming valve which became a key component in radios for nearly thirty years. This valve was also important to the development of televisions, telephones, and the earliest of computers. Fleming's groundbreaking work in the area of physics and engineering laid the basis for our modern field of electronics.

Max Planck, renowned German physicist and founder of the quantum theory

Louis Pasteur, rejecter of spontaneous generation and pioneer in preventive medicine, a biologist and chemist whose work with germs and microorganisms opened up new fields of scientific study

Robert Boyle, honored by many as the "father of modern chemistry"

Wernher van Braun, a scientific icon due to his work in the early stages of rocket development who is sometimes dubbed the "Father of Modern Rocketry"

Dr. Carl Linnaeus, pioneer in preventative medicine and creator of the modern system for categorizing plants and animals that laid the foundation for our modern science known as Taxonomy

James Clerk Maxwell, renowned, award winning physicist

Henrietta Leavitt, discoverer of the Period-Luminosity Relation which evolved into todays accepted method of measurement for the sizes and distances of stars

The above mentioned scientists, which includes many of the founders of *modern science* as well as scientists studying and practicing today, are only a few of the thousands of scientists who academically thrive—or thrived—in the realm of scientific society. They are/were all brilliant men, many included in the elite of their field, yet they have/had no problem accepting the biblical teaching that "in the beginning God created" and even believe that there is evidence in their specific fields of science that support this belief. Why then are our children and youth being taught that "only ignorant and unlearned Christians" still believe in a God who created?

Scopes Trial Propaganda

Another example of the rewriting of history to destroy belief in the Creator and his creation is the Scopes Trial. If you have not had the opportunity to watch the 1960 version of *Inherit the Wind*, you might want to check this film out from your local library. If the 1960 black and white version isn't available, perhaps they will have the 1999 version. This movie is watched by students nationwide as an ***educational film*** in science, history, and social study classes; and the students watching it are usually led to believe that the film was based on true facts—facts surrounding the infamous *Scopes' Trial.* Read the following true facts about the Scopes Trial before and after watching this movie and try to count the number of outright lies or twisting of truths you find. I promise . . . it will be eye-opening!

Actual history: (All material below taken from *Inherit the Wind: a Hollywood History of the Scopes Trial* by Dr. David N. Menton.)

Scopes was a physics and math teacher and a football coach, not a biology teacher. He merely substituted for the biology teacher the last two weeks of school when the teacher became sick.

The American Civil Liberties Union (ACLU) in New York City had advertised for a biology teacher who would be willing to be the pawn in testing the Butler Law, a law that prohibited the teaching of evolution in Tennessee public schools. So it wasn't the town's people who were on the witch hunt, it was the ACLU.

The ACLU and George Rappleyea, a mine operator from Dayton, Tennessee, were responsible for indicting John Scopes for teaching evolution in the classroom. In reality, Scopes never taught on evolution. He even skipped over the topic while reviewing the students for their final exam.

Scopes was never jailed for teaching evolution. Nor was he prosecuted for his courageous stand on behalf of evolution by religious fanatics as the film portrays.

There was no Reverend Brown, so there was obviously no Reverend Brown's daughter. They were both totally fictitious characters inserted with the seeming intention of making Christians look like foolish, ignorant, and backward people. Yet these are two of the most influential characters in the film where children and youth are concerned. Reverend Brown even goes so far as to curse his own daughter for not "disowning" her boyfriend, John Scopes. Incidentally, Scopes didn't have a girlfriend at that time in history, so obviously she was never mistreated by Bryan on the witness stand.

The conservative Christians of Dayton, Tennessee are portrayed as greedy, ignorant, closed-minded, and discourteous people. They even behave in a threatening manner towards the defense lawyers, the news media, and outsiders in general. Yet Darrow himself stated, "I don't know as I was ever in a community in my life where my religious ideas differed as widely from the great mass as I have found them since I have been in Tennessee. Yet I came here a perfect stranger and I can say what I have said before that I have not found upon any body's part—any citizen here in this town or outside the slightest discourtesy. I have been treated better, kindlier and more hospitably than I fancied would have been the case in the north."

Bryan was not ignorant of the teaching of evolution. In fact, he had written many well-argued articles which were critical of the scientific evidence used as proof of evolution in his day. He had long carried on a correspondence on the subject with the famous evolutionist, Henry Fairfield Osborn—the same Osborn who made the statement that if a hypothetical unbiased zoologist from Mars visited our planet he would classify people into several distinct groups or species. Osborn taught that the darker the person's skin, the less evolved to full human status that person was. In contrast, Darrow gave the impression of having a very poor grasp of both the meaning and mechanism of evolution.

The testimony of the evolutionists assembled by the defense was prevented because Darrow adamantly refused to allow them to be cross-examined by Bryan. After Bryan received permission of question them, Darrow never called them to the witness stand.

The definition of the term *evolution* was constantly muddled by the defense and its witnesses throughout the entire trial, even to the point that it would have been unlikely that the jurors could have understood what it truly meant. Remember, at that point in history it wasn't as widely taught in the educational system as it is today.

After spending the seventh day of the trial systematically grilling and ridiculing Bryan for his Christian beliefs, including the belief in the miracles of the Bible, Darrow abruptly ended the trial by asking the judge to instruct the jury to find his client guilty. There was a purpose for this. Bryan had only agreed to take the witness stand to answer questions on his Christian beliefs on the condition that he could then, in turn, question Darrow about his own agnostic and evolutionary beliefs. But with Darrow's conniving move of requesting his client's guilt, Bryan would never be allowed to examine Darrow. Also, he would not be allowed to give his closing argument, which was a well-supported scientific and religious argument against the theory of evolution.

In *Inherit the Wind*, when his client is found guilty (as Darrow requested), Darrow is visibly shaken by this great injustice. Bryan, on the other hand, is vindictive and argues bitterly that the $100.00 fine leveled against Scopes wasn't enough for a crime of such great magnitude. In reality, all of Scopes' expenses were covered by various interests, as was his tuition for a graduate education in geology after the trial finished. So he never spent time in jail, he wasn't persecuted, nor did the trial cost him a cent.

The entire purpose for the trial was to (a) declare the Butler Act unconstitutional, (b) expose fundamentalist Christian views on the subject of origins to public ridicule in the press, and (c) focus the attention of the world on evolution.

Never did Bryan lose his senses and begin crazily ranting in the courtroom, nor did he, while trying to recite the books of the Bible, fall dead on the courtroom floor. He died 5 days later while resting in a peaceful sleep.

"The Christian fundamentalists are consistently lampooned throughout the film, while skeptics and agnostics are consistently portrayed as intelligent, kindly and even heroic."

The writers obviously did not intend to write a historically accurate account of the Scopes trial, yet this is how it is presented in many of our school systems today.

Question: *Why do you think the world feels it necessary to belittle someone who believes the biblical story of creation?*

Tragic Truth: The Scopes Trial and Columbine

Besides the rewriting of history to make Christians who believe in the biblical version of creation seem ignorant and evolutionists seem intelligent, there are many other side effects to swallowing Darwin's theory as fact. In 1925, when the *Scopes Trial* enabled the widespread entrance of evolution into our school systems, the character of the classroom slowly began to change. This moral decline didn't happen overnight, because it takes time for moral decadence to work its way into the mainstream culture. "What could the teaching of evolution possibly have in common with the moral decline of a society?" you ask. Consider what this theory is based on: *Man is an accident. He came from nowhere, he's going nowhere, and life is a point of pain in a meaningless existence. So why not have fun while you can, before you become just a pile of dust?* Take a look at this survey which was conducted every 10 years beginning in 1969:

High school students were asked, "Have you ever lied to your parents about how you're doing in school?" In 1969 52% said they had. In 1979 the number increased to 60%. In 1989 the number increased again, this time to 71%. In 1999 84% of the students surveyed said they had lied to their parents about how they were doing in school.

When high school students in 1969 were asked if they had ever signed their parent's name to an excuse, 26% reported that they had. That number increased to 42% in 1979, 58% in 1989, and 73% in 1999.

In 1969 82% of the students agreed that "Honesty is the best policy." In 1969 89% of the students surveyed agreed that "Crime does not pay." By 1999 only 43% agreed with that statement.

Go to the following web site www.answersingenesis.org/creation/v25/i3/geraci.asp and read the article titled *Tragic Truth: Pastor Gino Geraci at Columbine and Ground Zero.*

Food for Thought: *Where do you see bias against Christianity in our media today?*

Chapter 2: The Bible and Creation

Suggested Reading: Chapter 2 in *The Case for a Creator*

Serious Theological Issues

Evolution teaches that our world is billions of years old, yet that's clearly opposite from the biblical creation story. So theologians who have swallowed evolution as fact have a problem, either they must agree that parts of the Bible are mythology, or they must come up with a means of inserting millions of years into Genesis chapter one.

Have you ever heard someone say, "Well, we don't know how long a day was in Genesis, after all, the Bible says that 'one day is as a thousand years' with God" (2 Peter 3:8). Besides the fact that you can't use a New Testament Greek definition to interpret an Old Testament Hebrew word (yom), that's taking 2 Peter 3:8 out of context. The apostle Peter's meaning is simply that God is outside the box of time. This is also seen in Psalm 90:4 which reads, "For a thousand years in your sight are like a day that has just gone by, all like a watch in the night." In both of these cases the context merely means that God is not limited by natural processes or time.

Or perhaps you've heard someone say, "Oh, I believe God created everything we see, but I believe that as God He could have used any means of creation that He wished. He could even have used evolution." That kind of thinking is the foundation of several theories that have been proposed in the last two hundred years in an attempt to mesh evolution into the creation story. These theories include the Gap Theory, Progressive Creation and Theistic Evolution. But biblically speaking is it really possible to insert millions of years into the creation story? Absolutely not! And here are some of the reasons why:

Evolution places Adam as the product of millions of years of death instead of its originator. This causes an extremely serious theological issue, because if the first Adam's sin isn't the cause of death, then neither can the Second Adam's sacrifice for sin bring the resurrection of life (1 Corinthians 15: 21-22). In other words, if evolution is true, the gospel is false. This means there is no resurrection from the dead, and when we die we turn to dust and are gone forever.

In the creation story plants were created on the third day, yet animals and man weren't created until day six. What do plants breathe in? Carbon dioxide. What do they give off? Oxygen. What do humans breathe in? Oxygen. What do we exhale? Carbon dioxide. This means that plants and humans (animals included) had to coexist in the environment in order for either to survive. If the days of creation were actually millions of years, the plants would have used up all of the carbon dioxide and died off long before man and animals came along to replenish it.

In Genesis 2:7 God says that Adam was made from the dust of the ground. An ape and dust are two very different things. Also, in Genesis 3:19 God informs Adam that after a hard life he would one day return to the dust from which he was taken. If the word *dust* actually means *ape*, then we would expect men to be turning back into apes upon their deaths. How many times have you seen that happen?

Where did Eve come from? If Adam was the product of millions of years of slow mutations, once he had finally fully mutated to human status, where did Eve come from? Did God use evolution by natural processes to create the male and then turn around and perform a miracle to create the woman? How much sense does that make? If God could perform a miracle to create Eve, could He not also have performed a miracle to create Adam?

At the end of the sixth day of creation God pronounced His creation *very good*. Yet if Adam was the product of millions of years of death, disease, violence, parasites, fungi, and bloodshed, which is what evolution teaches, and God called this *very good*, then what kind of a God do we serve? My idea of a good and loving God is not one who would pronounce millions of years of death *very good*. Besides, God promised to one day restore the earth back to its original state. If death was the means by which God originally created, then His restoration would be no different than what we see in our world today.

Note that Adam lived through the sixth and seventh days of creation before falling to temptation. If the days in Genesis were actually thousands or millions of years as some of these theories suggest, then how can the Bible state that he died at only 930 years of age? (Genesis 5:3)

Note that the sequence of events in the theory of evolution and the creation story are different. Evolution teaches that life first began in the sea and after millions of years moved up onto land. Yet the Bible teaches that God created the trees and plants before the fish in the sea and the birds of the air. Also, evolution teaches that the earth first began as a hot molten blob, yet the Bible teaches that upon its creation it was covered with water.

Jesus, who is given the credit for the creation of all, stated that "from the *beginning* He created them male and female."

Finally, if the days of creation were really millions of years instead of solar days, then God isn't a very good writer. Let me explain this statement.

The Hebrew word for day (yom) can have a variety of meanings. It can mean a solar day, daylight (sun up to sundown), and a period of time, such as "In my father's day." So the question we need to answer is which definition did God mean when inspiring Moses to pen the creation story? Let's examine this question by moving outside of Genesis chapter one since that is the chapter in question. How are *yom,* and its plural *yamin,* usually used in the Old Testament passages, and are there any guidelines by which the words are used?

The guidelines to follow with the word *yom* are, whenever it is used in the Old Testament with the words "evening" or "morning" or with a numeral or ordinal in a historical narrative, it is always, without fail, a reference to a solar day. *Yamin*, on the other hand, never has any other meaning except a set of literal solar days.

Now let's insert these guidelines into Genesis 1. Repeatedly we read the phrase "and the evening and morning were the ___ day." Both of the words *evening* and *morning* are present, as well as an ordinal 1st, 2nd, etc.. This makes the chronological order of Genesis 1 very tight, not an indefinite period of time.

Let's also take a look at Exodus 20:8-11. Remember it was Moses who wrote the first five books of the Bible (called the Pentateuch) under the inspiration of God, but the *10 Commandments* were written by the very finger of God. So what does God write in these tablets? "Remember the Sabbath *yom,* to keep it holy. Six *yamin* you shall labor and do all your work, but the seventh *yom* is the Sabbath of the LORD your God. In it you shall do no work . . . For in six *yamin* the LORD made the heavens and the earth, the sea, and all that is in them, and rested the seventh *yom*. Therefore the LORD blessed the Sabbath *yom* and made it holy."

Remember that *yamin* always, without fail, means solar days. So there is no other way to interpret Exodus 20 than to say that God created the world in six literal solar days.

Also, the word *remember* in verse 8 is a Hebrew word that always refers back to a real historical event. And the word *for* in verse 11 is usually translated *because* and also always refers back to a real event. Again, what did God write about this real historical event with His own finger? He very clearly wrote that our world was created in six literal solar days.

Conclusion: *God equates the six days of creation with our six day work week. From this we can conclude that, if God can write clearly, then our world was created in six solar days. Since God is omnipotent, my question would be, "Why did He take so long?"*

What Does the Bible Actually Teach?

Teachers: Complete the worksheet *Chapter 2: What Does the Bible Actually Teach* before continuing.

John 1:1-3 and Colossians 1:15-18—These verses reveal that Jesus is God incarnate, meaning God in the flesh. He is called the Word, and it was through Him that everything created was created. In Colossians 1:15-18 Paul presents Christ as Creator, coeternal with the Father and over even the highest orders of heaven and earth. John 1:14 further clarifies the fact that Christ is God incarnate by declaring that the Word became flesh and dwelt among men. The Greek word for Word here is Logos, which carries the idea of a unique communication of God to man.

Psalms 33:6-9—God SPOKE His creation into being. He didn't take a lump of clay like a potter would need to create a finished product, He merely spoke and all that is seen and unseen in the universe came into being—all except man.

Mark 10:3-6—Jesus, creator of all, stated that from the very "beginning of creation" God made them male and female. Who else would know better the method, sequence and timing of creation than the Creator himself?

Genesis 2:7—God didn't speak man into existence as He did the rest of creation. Instead, He took dust from the ground and formed Adam's body and then He breathed the breath of life into his nostrils. At the moment God's breath entered Adam's body, man became a living being.

Genesis 1:31—God gives us the exact chronological order of His creation, and man lands on day six. Take note for a later discussion that when God finished the creation of man He declared his work "very good." Since this declaration was made on the actual day of man's creation, there was nothing Adam could have done to earn this decree. God declared him "very good" based on His opinion alone. This helps us to understand that our significance comes from our Creator not from our performance, our opinion, or even the opinions of others.

Romans 5:12 and 1 Corinthians 15:21-22—Sin entered the world through one man's sin, and death through sin. As a result, all of mankind inherited a sin nature and is destined to experience both physical and spiritual death. Yet God's love for us was so strong that He sent the Second Adam, the Lord Jesus Christ, to pay the wages for our sin on Calvary so that we could be reunited with Him.

Second Peter 3:3-6—Peter prophesized that in the end times scoffers would come, mocking the idea that Christ would return for His own. These mockers would also willfully choose to forget that the world was created by the spoken word of God, and that the earth was destroyed with water during the flood of Noah's day. Is this what we see today? Absolutely. The theory of evolution is taught instead of the story of creation, and even though there are millions of fossils that give evidence that great flood waters once covered the earth, Noah's flood is often repeated as one of those "cute little Bible myths."

Romans 8:22—When Adam fell, God's entire creation suffered. "All of creation groans and labors with pangs" awaiting the coming of the Savior. Why does even nature await the coming of Christ? Because Christ's redemptive work at Calvary extends even to the sin-cursed cosmos itself, meaning that one day God will restore nature to its pre-fall (Garden of Eden) condition.

Acts 3:20-21—Again, God has appointed a time when all of creation will be restored to its original perfect state of being.

1 Corinthians 15:45-49—Even as the first Adam became a living being, the Last Adam (Christ) became a life-giving Spirit so that all who trust in Him will not be held in bondage to the power of sin. Instead, we will be reunited with God in eternity. And even though we were originally born of the dust of the ground, in eternity we will bear the image of Christ in glorified bodies.

Does the Bible Date Man?

Having established the fact that the Bible does indeed teach that God created the heavens and earth and all that is in them in six solar days, is there any evidence as to how far back in time this event occurred? Yes, there is. Genesis gives us the actual timetable of the early generations of man. Some people try to claim that only key names were mentioned, therefore our record of years fall drastically short of reality, but this simply does not fit the scriptures. Why? Because God gave us the exact age that each person was when their son who is mentioned was born.

For instance, in Genesis 5, 7, and 11 we discover that Adam was 130 years old when his son Seth was born; Seth was 105 when Enosh was born; Enosh was 90 when Cainan was born; Cainan was 70 when Mahalaleel was born; Mahalaleel was 65 when Jared was born; Jared was 162 when Methusaleh was born; Methusaleh was 187 when Lamech was born; Lamech was 182 when Noah was born; Noah was 600 when the flood destroyed the earth and two years after leaving the ark his grandson Arphaxad was born; Arphaxad was 35 when Shelah was born; Shelah was 30 when Eber (from where we believe the word Hebrew comes) was born; Eber was 34 when Peleg was born; Peleg was 30 when Reu was born; Reu was 32 when Serug was born; Serug was 30 when Nahor was born; Nahor was 29 when Terah was born; and Terah was 70 when Abraham (the father of the Jewish race) was born. Using other data to date backward in time, the *estimated* birth for Abraham was about 2166 B.C. This doesn't leave any room for the additional hundreds of thousands of years to be inserted into the creation of man to make it compatible with the theory of evolution.

Also, in the New Testament book of Jude, written by one of Jesus' half-brothers (Matt. 13:55; Mark 6:3), we read that there were seven generations from Enoch to Adam. This again eliminates this theory that many generations passed between each name and that only key names were recorded. Although we're not given enough data to know the exact number of years from the creation of Adam and Eve until present day, we are given enough to know that it was somewhere around 6000 years.

You might be surprised to discover that there is scientific evidence (assuming the calculations and original assumptions were correct) to support a much more recent entrance of man into the creation picture than evolution allows. The study of genetics is a relatively new science, yet with the more recent advancements in this field creationists have yet another weapon in their arsenal. Let me explain. Today, like never before, a person can be convicted in a court of law when there were no witnesses simply because of the presence of their genetic makeup, their DNA, at a crime scene. Also, if an unrecognizable body is found, its DNA can be compared to a prospective family member to verify its identity. The DNA exclusively found in females, mitochondrial DNA, can be used to identify daughter to mother, mother to grandmother, grandmother to great-grandmother, and so on.

How does this mitochondrial DNA add another weapon into the biblical date of creation? When a group of researchers originally traced the female mitochondrial DNA backward, they discovered that every female on this planet came from one original woman, whom they appropriately named Mitochondrial Eve. In this research they estimated that Mitochondrial Eve lived approximately 200,000 years ago. But then a mistake was discovered in the original mutation rate calculations, and when their figures were refigured with the correct information (again assuming it is now correct) they estimated that Mitochondrial Eve lived a mere 6000 to 6500 years ago.

The DNA common to all men is called Y-chromosome, and when it was placed into these same calculations the findings were the same as with Mitochondrial Eve. All men on this planet are descendants of one man, appropriately named Y-Chromosome Adam, who lived around 6000 to 6500 years ago.

This research is rejected by evolutionists because it doesn't fit their world view, but it fits perfectly with the biblical dating of the creation of one man and one woman somewhere around 6000 years ago. In fact, this Y Chromosome Adam and Mitochondrial Eve time frame is far more biblically accurate than some theologians who have tried to mesh evolution into the creation story (www.a-voice.org/qa/theistic.htm#eve).

Question: *Why do you suppose Christians sometimes compromise the teachings of the Bible?*

Biblical Questions often Raised about Genesis

Why do Genesis 1 and 2 seem to not fit chronologically?

Answer: Some have tried to argue that Genesis 1 and 2 contradict each other concerning the order of events during creation, but this simply is not true. The difference between these two chapters is this: Genesis 1 gives us a detailed chronological account of the order of God's creation, while Genesis 2 is a detailed unfolding of the same information but with an emphasis on God's relationship to His creation—man.

It presupposes chapter 1 and is complementary and supplementary, not contradictory.

Actually, the events in Genesis 1 are much like a drama. In the first three days of creation the backdrop of the drama was set in place: the heavens and earth, light and darkness, waters on the earth divided from the waters above (atmosphere), and land and vegetation appear. On days four, five and six the characters of the drama arrive on scene: the solar system, the fish in the seas and the birds in the air, and the animals and man.

Where did Cain get his wife?

Read Genesis 4 and answer the following questions.

Do verses 16-17 say that Cain went to the land of Nod to *find a wife,* or that he *knew* his wife and she conceived and bore a son?

What was Cain's response to God's discipline?

Is there anything about Cain's response that would not fit with the idea that he and his parents were the only living humans at that time on planet earth?

The name Seth is used eight times in the entire Bible. Look up these verses in a Bible translation (not a paraphrased Bible but a real translation) and write down every detail about Seth that is mentioned. Take note specifically if you find the number "3" or the ordinal "3rd" mentioned in any of these verses. Genesis 4:25—

Genesis 4:26—

Genesis 5:3—

Genesis 5:4—

Genesis 5:6—

Genesis 5:7—

Genesis 5:8—

Luke 3:38—

Summary: If you read these references in a Bible translation and not a man's paraphrased version, you should have noticed that the ordinal "3rd" was never mentioned. Seth is recorded as being the "righteous son who took righteous Abel's place." People often refer to him as Adam and Eve's 3rd son, but that is nowhere stated in the scriptures. Also, notice in Genesis 5:3 that Seth wasn't born until Adam was 130 years old. After that Adam lived another 800 years and had "sons and daughters."

At the time of Josephus, a quite reliable Jewish historian, Jewish tradition taught that Adam and Eve had 55 children, 23 daughters and 32 sons. In the *Book of Jubilee* it records Cain's wife as being a daughter of Adam and Eve named Awan.

Now go back to what didn't seem right with Cain's complaint to God. When he said, ". . . and it will happen that anyone who finds me will kill me," the LORD responded, "Therefore, whoever kills Cain, vengeance shall be taken on him sevenfold." Then it continues to read, "And the LORD set a mark on Cain, lest anyone finding him should kill him."

So the question to be asked is, "Who is anyone?" If Adam and Eve were the only people alive at that time, of whom was Cain afraid? Surely Adam and Eve would not have killed their only remaining living son. The second question would be, "And where did Cain get his wife?" These verses say that upon receiving God's curse Cain went out from the presence of the LORD (which was probably a reference to away from the area where the Garden of Eden was still located), traveled to the land of Nod and knew his wife so that she bore their first son, Enoch.

The mistake usually made is to assume that because Seth is the 3rd son of Adam and Eve *mentioned in the scriptures*, he is also their *3rd son born*. Yet nowhere in scripture is Seth identified as the 3rd child born to Adam and Eve. Why then, out of Adam and Eve's assumed 55 children, were Cain, Abel, and Seth the only ones mentioned specifically by name? First, Cain was mentioned because he was their first born son and became the first murderer. Second, Abel is mentioned because he became the first victim of murder. And third, Seth is mentioned because he is the "son who took righteous Abel's place" and was destined to be the ancestral father of the promised Messiah. In other words, there was a specific reason for the Lord mentioning these three sons over the other children.

When you take away the assumption that Seth was Adam and Eve's 3rd son, everything fits together perfectly in the Bible story. Cain was already married to Awan at the time of the murder of Abel, and upon God's judgment moved away from his relatives and to the land of Nod where his first son was born. Seth, clearly born after Abel's murder, was born 130 years after Adam and Eve had been having children, so he wasn't their 3rd child, but merely the "son who took righteous Abel's place."

Question: *What lies concerning evolution have you been taught as scientific fact?*

Chapter 3: Why Study Evolution?

Suggested Reading: Chapter 3 in *The Case for a Creator*

Why Should Christians Study Evolution?

Have you ever heard someone say, "But we're Bible believing Christians, why should we study a theory that counters the Scriptures?" If we are to prepare our youth for that charismatic, atheist professor who thrives on ripping all faith away, we must study this theory. What commander ever goes to war without having studied his opponent? And don't kid yourself; creation and evolution are at war. G. Richard Bozarth, in the American Atheist (Feb. 1978, pp. 19, 30) wrote:

Christianity has fought, still fights, and will fight science to the desperate end over evolution, because evolution destroys utterly and finally the very reason Jesus' earthly life was supposedly made necessary. Destroy Adam and Eve and the original sin, and in the rubble you will find the sorry remains of the son of god...If Jesus was not the redeemer who died for our sins, and this is what evolution means, then Christianity is nothing!"

Even an atheist can understand that if Adam and Eve were the product of millions of years of death, disease and violence (evolution at its finest), then they were not the founders of death due to their sin as the Bible teaches. You can't have it both ways!

We are indeed at war! And like the commander of any army, we need to know our enemy. Paul stated in 2 Timothy 2:15 that we should always be able to give an account for what we believe. Time and time again, I've heard the sad stories of individuals who were raised to believe in God, yet because the adult Christians around them were unable to answer simple questions in defense of the Christian faith, they were swayed to believe the teachings of evolutionists and eventually slipped out the back doors of the church a proclaimed atheist.

For example, the evolutionary entomologist and sociobiologist E. Wilson said, "When I was fifteen, I entered the Southern Baptist Church with great fervor and interest in the fundamentalist religion; I left at seventeen when I got to the University of Alabama and heard about evolutionary theory."

Besides being able to give an answer for what we believe, we also need to know our enemy for witnessing purposes. In the past 200 years Satan has used this mighty evolutionary tool so effectively that he has removed the existence of a divine creator from the minds of many. They've swallowed evolutionists' lie that the Bible was proven false years ago by science, and until that belief is corrected they won't be open to the gospel message. That's why we must refute these lies both biblically and intellectually (scientifically), so we can be a lighthouse for Christ to a lost and dying world.

Teachers: Complete Worksheet *Chapter 3: Why Should Christians Study Evolution?*

Refuting Evolutionist's Lies

Origin of science?

Since science was developed in Christian Europe by men who assumed that an orderly God would have created an orderly universe, there would be no reason to expect order in nature if God didn't created an orderly universe and instead it is merely the product of random chance. (Paterson 20)

What is science?

As stated before, there are two types of science, operational and historical. Operational science must be observable with one or more of our five senses or experimentally repeatable so that it can be tested and potentially falsifiable. It involves testing and verifying ideas in the present and leads to the production of useful products. Historical science involves interpreting evidence from the past, and when you recognize that everyone has presupposed philosophical ideas that bias their interpretations, it helps you to understand that historical science is not equal to operational science.

Is evolution science?

Again, since evolution is not directly observable, testable, or repeatable, it is historical science and not operational science. It is based upon philosophical assumptions about how the universe began (Big-Band theory), and any time your founding assumptions abandon God, your conclusion will too. That's why evolutionists who study the same evidence as creationists will end with a totally different conclusion. They started with a bias, that evolution is true, so their conclusion would obviously support that bias.

Is evolution fact?

It is also important to understand that there are two very different definitions for the word evolution, and these definitions are in no way equal. For instance, evolution can be used in the sense of small changes within a species by natural selection, which is often referred to as microevolution and is accepted by evolutionists and creationists alike as good operational science. The Bible even supports this kind of evolution. When Noah and his family left the ark after the global flood, at least two of every kind of animal left with them. Each of these sets of "kinds" began breeding within their kind, and as the decades passed variety among each kind developed.

Example: Noah took two dogs, one male and one female, aboard the ark. The genetic makeup of those two dogs contained all the information necessary for the variety of dogs that we see in our world today. That's variation within a species—microevolution. What the Bible does not teach is macroevolution, which involves the idea that all organisms on earth share one common ancestor by descent with modification. It is not the amount of change that is different, but its type and direction. Microevolution involves a loss of information in the genetic pool, while macroevolution involves an addition to that information—and that is what has never been proven. The confusion arises because these two definitions of evolution are often used interchangeably, as though they were one and the same. Textbooks deceptively use microevolution examples to argue that macroevolution, in the molecules-to-man sense, must have occurred. Yet variation within a species or kind cannot be used as evidence that all kinds evolved from one common ancestor. No matter how many millennium you tack onto the equation, a frog will never become a prince.

What do the laws of science teach?

First we must understand the difference between laws and theories. For instance, there is a force that tends to draw all bodies in the earth's sphere toward the center of the earth. This force is called the *law of gravity*, and laws cannot be broken without outside assistance. For example, if you jump off the edge of the Grand Canyon what is going to happen? Splat! Ten years from now if you jump off the edge of the Grand Canyon what will be the result? Splat! Ten million years from now if you jump off the edge of the Grand Canyon what will happen? Splat again. That's because without outside interference, such as an aircraft, gravity will always pull you toward the center of the earth. Theories on the other hand are speculative ideas as to how something might have happened. If that speculative idea is one day proven to be fact, then it is no longer a theory but a law. Ever wonder why the theory of evolution is called just that, the *theory of evolution*? It's because it has never been proven to be a law.

The difference between laws and theories is extremely significant when dealing with evolution. Why? Because several of the laws of science actually defy the theory of evolution. Yes, the laws of science defy the theory that all life mutated from one original cell. Let's take a look at some of these laws.

Law of Biogenesis—the law of biogenesis (spontaneous generation) states that life always comes from life. This law, in reversed wording, states that life never comes from nonlife and was proven by Lewis Pasteur. Also included in the law of biogenesis is *mutation to transmutation*, which states that mutations in nature never go uphill. This means there is never an increase in genetic information when a mutation takes place; it is always a loss of information or a mistake in the doubling of the genetic makeup that is already present within the animal. Good examples of this "repeat of already present information" are frequently found and often used as "evidence" of macroevolution, although they are the exact opposite. When you see a calf with an extra leg, or a cat with four ears, it is always a repeat of already present genetic information that was somehow messed up during development. Never do you see new information, such as a fish accidently gaining the information necessary to grow feathers, occur naturally; yet the theory of evolution depends entirely upon this concept.

Cause and effect—a design always implies a designer. If you have a cake, you have a cake baker; if you have a watch, you have a watch maker; and if you have a universe, you have a universe creator.

2nd Law of Thermodynamics—the 2nd law of thermodynamics states that everything in the universe is going to a lower state of energy, not a higher state. Again, this means a decrease in information, not an addition to it.

Law of Motion—the law of motion states that something never comes from nothing in regard to energy. If a leaf blows across your yard, there was energy behind that movement. It is impossible for the leaf to blow itself, yet that is exactly what evolution teaches. Assuming the Big-Bang really occurred, what caused it? What was the energy behind the movement that caused our universe to suddenly come into existence?

Law of probability—Did you know there is an actual number that represents the impossible? "The laws of statistics show that favorable mutations are so improbable that they will most likely never even happen *once* in twenty billion years, let alone happen millions of times. The laws of science absolutely preclude evolution, pointing towards degradation of life's complex systems, and not toward evolutionary integration" (Morris 41).

Exactly how probable is it that all of life evolved from nonlife? Consider the fact that "Human DNA contains more organized information than the Encyclopedia Britannica" (Strobel 219). Actually, the amount of information in the Encyclopedia Britannica pales in comparison to the amount of information in one human cell, yet evolutionists explain this enormous amount of information as the workings of random forces. "If the full text of the Britannica Encyclopedias were to arrive in computer code from outer space," who in their right mind would consider it the workings of random chance (Strobel 219)? Most people would regard it as proof of the existence of extraterrestrial intelligence. (*The impossibility of evolution actually occurring will be discussed in more detail in a further topic.*)

Frauds of Evolution

Perhaps one of the best known and effective illustrations when marketing the theory of evolution is a picture we've all seen, the picture of an ape on the left side of the drawing who—by the time you reach the right side of the drawing—has evolved into full human status. This picture has been portrayed in science books for years to help support the teaching of molecules to ape to man evolution.

Along with this picture were examples, or missing links, that were presented as no longer missing. These missing links were pushed as further evidence that man had indeed evolved from ape. Let's take a better look at some of these so-called missing links, some of which are even today used as evidence to bolster the theory of evolution.

Java Man—Java man was dug up in 1891 by the Dutch scientist Eugene Dubois on an Indonesian Island. He was dubbed "the missing link" by Dubois even though he was nothing more than a skullcap, a femur, three teeth, and a great deal of artistic imagination. (Strobel 61)

Neanderthals—Neanderthals were once believed to be cave-dwelling brutes that were less than human status. We often see him in cartoons grabbing his prospective Mrs. Neanderthal by her matted hair and dragging her to his home, which of course is a cave. This less-than-human status was based on a slight difference in some of their bone structures, which may well have been caused by disease and lack of proper nutrition due to their harsh living environment. Some evolutionists are even now admitting that they were as human as you and I. (Patterson 231-233)

Piltdown Man—Piltdown Man was a deliberate hoax pawned off as proof of evolution for over 50 years. Finally, when two scientists gained permission to examine his skeletal remains more closely, it was discovered that he was created from a piece of an ape's jaw and the skull of a human, all artificially aged. Why did it take over 50 years for this fraud to be discovered? I believe it was because evolutionist scientists so wanted to believe the missing link had finally been found, that there was proof to support their belief, that he was accepted as authentic without scrutiny (Patterson 229).

Nebraska Man—Nebraska Man, his wife, and his children were all created from one tooth and an enormous amount of imagination. Talk about artistic creativity! How could anyone draw an entire family of never-seen-before creatures from one tooth? Yet that was Mr. Nebraska Man's origin. Finally, when someone got a hold of the tooth who knew what he was doing, he identified it as the tooth of an extinct pig. Again, the extreme desire for evolution to be true tainted the conclusion, causing a false missing link to be pushed without scrutiny (Patterson 227). Interesting note: "When the National Geographic hired four artists to reconstruct a female figure from seven fossil bones found in Kenya, they came up with quite different interpretations. One looked like a modern African-American woman; another like a werewolf; another had a heavy, gorilla-like brow; and another had a missing forehead and jaws that looked a little like a beaked dinosaur. . . . One anthropologist likened the task to trying to reconstruct the plot of *War and Peace* by using just thirteen random pages from the book" (Strobel 62). Yet this is exactly what evolutionists do and call it science!

Lucy—Lucy was discovered by Louis Leakey's team of excavators in 1959. She is a grossly ape-like skeleton that is one of the most often cited examples of the missing link. Leakey dubbed her the missing link, not because of any skeletal evidence proving she was part human and part ape, but because she was found with tools nearby. He assumed those tools to belong to her. His son, Richard Leakey, after his father's death, returned to that same cave in hopes of expounding further upon his father's discovery, but instead of adding clout to Lucy as the missing link, his further excavation dethroned her forever. Beneath the spot where her skeletal remains were found years earlier, a human skeleton was discovered. Obviously, the tools which had led to her being hailed as the missing link belonged to humans. At the time, Richard Leakey said his discovery shattered standard beliefs in evolution (Patterson 230).

"Actually, fossil discoveries have been shattering standard beliefs in evolution with monotonous regularity. Each in its day was hailed as 'scientific proof' that human beings evolved from apelike animals, yet all the candidates once proposed as our evolutionary ancestors have been knocked off the list or are in serious question—meaning not proven. The cover story in *Time Magazine* for March 14, 1994, assumes that evolution is an absolute fact, yet turns around and summarizes an evaporating case for human evolution" (Strobel 62).

Now, in 2009, evolutionists are once again claiming to have finally discovered the missing link. Her name is Ida. According to one report Ida is the "latest and greatest" missing link ever discovered. Another reporter raved, "The search for a direct connection between humans and the rest of the animal kingdom has taken 200 years—but it was presented to the world today at a special news conference in New York." When I first heard about this "latest and greatest missing link finds," I knew that Ida would one day fall from her throne; that she, too, would either be proven to be a complete fraud, a very creative artist's predisposed idea, or nothing more than some type of extinct ape. When we hear of findings like Ida, we've got to train ourselves to remember that historical science includes assumptions, and if the assumptions are wrong then so is the conclusion. Whenever historical science counters the teaching of God's word, we can rest assured that something is wrong with the original assumptions that led to the false conclusion.

Question: *If you have been taught by a public school science teacher who believed in the theory of evolution, how did that teacher respond if a student questioned evolution in your class?*

Chapter 4: A Closer Look

Suggested Reading: Chapter 4 in *The Case for a Creator*

In the beginning God

My how the times have changed! Since ancient time secular science has always assumed the universe to be eternal, making Christians seem foolish to believe the earth had a beginning, a time when God spoke its existence into being. Even back only 100 years ago Christians had to maintain their faith in the Bible in spite of all appearances. But now, as Craig pointed out in *The Case for a Creator,* "It is the atheist who has to maintain by faith, despite all of the evidence to the contrary, that the universe did not have a beginning a finite time ago" (Strobel 120). So the table has now turned. It is the Christian belief that is bolstered by science and the atheist who is left looking foolish.

Evidence from across a wide range of sciences that has come to the forefront in only the past few decades provides a robust case for believing in a Creator. In fact, many scientists are becoming believers in a Creator as a direct result of their studies. Even atheists have taken note of the evidence of intelligence behind creation, but rather than admit in a God who created, they have devised a new concept, a secular intelligent designer. In the documentary recently released by Ben Stein, *Expelled: No Intelligence Allowed,* Richard Dawkins, an outspoken atheist actor, makes the suggestion that perhaps life was delivered to our planet by "highly-evolved aliens," or maybe even "on the backs of diamonds." Now you tell me which takes more faith, to believe highly developed aliens or diamonds delivered life to our planet, or to believe in a God who created? Dawkins skirted around the issue that his suggestions don't solve the "intelligent design" problem. After all, let's suppose he's correct and either highly-developed aliens or diamonds did carry life to this planet, from where did those aliens (or the life that was carried on the backs of diamonds) originate? He's back to the original problem. His suggestions went nowhere for he circled back to the original problem, from where did life first come?

Read John 1:1-18 and answer the following questions.

Compare John 1:1 & 18 with Genesis 1:2. What do we learn about God through these verses?

   What part of the Trinity (God in three Persons) does John refer to as the Word?

   What evidence/verses did you base your previous answer on?

   Who does the Bible give credit for all of creation?

   Darkness is the absence of what?

Genesis 1:1 begins with, "In the beginning God . . ."

   Explain the concept *Design = Designer* and give an illustration to support your explanation.

   How would you answer someone who used the following statement to support their belief that there is no God? "You say every design must have a designer. Doesn't that mean God must have had a beginning too?" (Strobel 104-109)

What would be the characteristics of a Cause with the intelligence to create a universe like ours? (Strobel 108)

According to Craig on page 99 of *The Case for a Creator*, what is a key problem for atheists?

Finish the following quote: "Stephen Hawking has said, 'Almost everyone now believes that the universe, and time itself, had a beginning at the _____.'" (Strobel 107)

Continue with the following questions over Genesis 1:1. "In the beginning God created the heavens and the earth."

What does the Hebrew word *ex nihilo* mean? (Strobel 77)

"Created" is the Hebrew word "bara." It is exclusively used with God as its subject, indicating that only God could accomplish the act of creating something from nothing. It also carries the idea of an instantaneous and miraculous creation. How does this fit into your reading of Bill Bryson's comment in *A Short History of Nearly Everything* found in your text on page 94?

In Genesis 1:3 we read, "Then God said . . ." How does this correlate with what we previously learned from Psalm 33:6-9?

Genesis 1:21 reads, "So God created the great creatures of the sea and every living and moving thing with which the water teems, according to their kinds, and every winged bird according to its kind. And God saw that it was good" (NIV). Explain how the phrase "according to its kind" counters the theory of evolution.

Genesis 1:26 reads, "Then God (Elohim) said, 'Let Us make man in Our image, in Our likeness, and let them rule over the fish of the sea and the birds of the air, over the livestock, over all the earth, and over all the creatures that move along the ground'" (NIV).

What four references to the Trinity are in this one verse?

This verse uses the Hebrew word "yasar" which means "to fashion" and pictures God a potter meticulously shaping and forming man and breathing into him the breath of life. How is man's creation different from the rest of God's creation?

After the creation of man, for the first time, we see the name *LORD God* used (Genesis 2:4). This name, *Yahweh,* is God's covenant name. It is His name that is used in reference to redemption. Why do you suppose God didn't reveal His redemptive nature until the creation of man?

Up until Genesis 2:4 the phrase "heavens and earth" is used, but in verse 4 God reverses the order to "earth and heavens." Why do you suppose, once again after the creation of man, that God reverses the order and places earth first?

Why do you suppose God didn't reveal His redemptive nature until the creation of man?

Question: *What do you think about actor Richard Dawkins' suggestion that life was either carried to this planet "on the backs of diamonds" or "by aliens"?*

Answers:

Compare John 1:1 & 14 with Genesis 1:2. What do we learn about God through these verses? *(Answer: The Hebrew name for God used in Genesis 1:1 is 'Elohim, which is plural in form but singular in number. This is the first teaching of what Christians refer to as the Trinity—God is three persons. John 1:1 & 14 further establish the existence of Christ, the 2nd Person in the Trinity, before the beginning of creation, and actually declares Him as none other than God himself. Genesis 1:2 then introduces us to the Spirit of God, the 3rd person of the Trinity. This is fully seen in Matthew 28:19 when Jesus instructs His disciples to "Go therefore and make disciples of all nations, baptizing them in the name of the Father, the Son, and the Holy Spirit.")*

What part of the Trinity (God in three persons) does John refer to as the Word? *(Answer: Jesus)*

What evidence/verses did you base your previous answer on? *(Answer: Verses 7, 10, 11, 14, 15, 17)*

Who does the Bible give credit for all of creation? *(Answer: Jesus)*

Darkness is the absence of what? (Answer: Light)

Genesis 1:1 begins with, "In the beginning God . . ."

Explain the concept *Design = Designer* and give an illustration to support your explanation. *(Answer: When you see any kind of intelligent design, it means there had to be a designer. Examples: a cake means there's a cake baker; a watch equals a watch maker; a universe equals a universe creator.)*

How would you answer someone who used the following statement to support their belief that there is no God? "You say every design must have a designer. Doesn't that mean God must have had a beginning too?" (Strobel 104-109) *(Answer: The Kalam argument states that whatever began to exist has a cause. Since the character of a Cause who could create our universe must be beyond space and time, God has always been. In other words, He didn't begin to exist at any finite time in the past, therefore He needs no cause. This isn't giving God special treatment, because atheists have long maintained that the universe can be eternal and uncaused. Strobel 109)*

What would be the characteristics of a Cause with the intelligence to create a universe like ours? (Strobel 108) *(The Cause would have to be uncaused, beginningless, timeless, spaceless, immaterial, a personal being endowed with freedom of will and enormous power. Sound familiar?)*

According to Craig on page 99 of *The Case for a Creator*, what is a key problem for atheists? *(Answer: Evolutionist's key problem is, if the universe had a beginning, which is believed by nearly all scientists now, then it couldn't have just popped into existence out of nothing and without a cause.)*

Finish the following quote: "Stephen Hawking has said, 'Almost everyone now believes that the universe, and time itself, had a beginning at the Big Bang.'" (Strobel 107)

Let's continue Genesis 1:1. "In the beginning God created the heavens and the earth." Answer the questions about the creation of the universe?

What does the Hebrew word *ex nihilo* mean? (Strobel 77) *(Answer: Created out of nothing.)*

"Created" is the Hebrew word "bara." It is exclusively used with God as its subject, indicating that only God could accomplish the act of creating something from nothing. It also carries the idea of an instantaneous and miraculous creation. How does this fit into your reading of Bill Bryson's comment in *A Short History of Nearly Everything* found in your text on page 94? *(Answer: His description of an instantaneous universe where 98% of matter there is or will ever be was created in 3 minutes is nothing but instant and miraculous as the word 'bara' indicated.)*

In Genesis 1:3 we read, "Then God said . . ." How does this correlate with what we previously learned from Psalm 33:6-9? *(Answer: God spoke and the universe and all it contains came into being.)*

Genesis 1:21 reads, "So God created the great creatures of the sea and every living and moving thing with which the water teems, according to their kinds, and every winged bird according to its kind. And God saw that it was good" (NIV). Explain how the phrase "according to its kind" counters the theory of evolution. *(Answer: Evolution teaches that all life evolved from one common ancestor, yet God says each will produce only after its own kind—which is exactly what we see in nature.)*

Genesis 1:26 reads, "Then God ('Elohim') said, 'Let Us make man in Our image, in Our likeness, and let them rule over the fish of the sea and the birds of the air, over the livestock, over all the earth, and over all the creatures that move along the ground'" (NIV).

What are the four references to the Trinity in this one verse?

The Hebrew word for **God** is 'Elohim' which is plural in form; God said "Let **Us** . . . **Our** image . . . **Our** likeness . . . This is again a direct teaching of the Trinity of three in One.

This verse uses the Hebrew word "yasar" which means "to fashion" and pictures God as a potter meticulously shaping and forming man and breathing into him the breath of life. How is man's creation different from the rest of God's creation? *(Answer: God breathed His own breath into Adam, but He merely spoke the rest of creation into existence.)*

After the creation of man, for the first time, we see the name LORD God used (Genesis 2:4). This name, *Yahweh,* is God's covenant name. It is His name that is used in reference to redemption.

Up until Genesis 2:4 the phrase "heavens and earth" is used, but in verse 4 God reverses the order to "earth and heavens." Why do you suppose, once again after the creation of man, that God reverses the order and places earth first? *(Answer: After man's creation the focus was switched from the rest of creation to the place where man dwelt. As LORD God Redeemer, God's interest centered on our little planet because that was the spot where the mystery of salvation would one day be settled.)*

Why do you suppose God didn't reveal His redemptive nature until the creation of man? *(Answer: God loves man and foreknew of Adam's sin in the garden. Revelation 13:8 and Hebrews 4:3 reveal that God had already designed our redemption through Christ's sacrifice before the foundation of the world. He foreknew man, His most precious creation, would need a Redeemer and therefore became that Redeemer.)*

Your opinion . . .

Teachers: Complete worksheet Chapter 4: Creation Versus Evolution—Puzzle 1

Chapter 5: Dating History

Suggested Reading: Chapter 5 & 6 in *The Case for a Creator*

Talking Rocks?

Have you ever read an article or heard a news report that went something like this, "A local university professor discovers a 640 million year old rock, once again giving proof that Darwin's theory of evolution is true"? If you have, did you wonder where they came up with that age? Was the rock discovered with a tag dating it at 640 million years old? Or did the rock perhaps talk, telling the discoverer its age? I wish I could tell you that no one actually believes rock are alive, but I'm afraid I would be wrong. When I was in college I met a young lady who was a rock activist. "How silly," you say. "Rocks aren't alive. They can't talk." And you're obviously right, rocks aren't alive and they don't talk. So where then do they come up with these prehistoric dates?

John D. Morris, in his book *The Young Earth,* gives an excellent illustration of the method many scientists use to date rocks and fossils. He uses the classroom setting where a student brings a sedimentary rock (limestone) containing a fossil to his professor and requests the professor to date it. The professor indicates that it is entirely possible to date this specific rock because of a fossil that is preserved in it. He then goes over and picks up a huge invertebrate paleontology book, locates the fossil in the book that closest matches the fossil in the rock, and proceeds to give the rock a date—640 million years. Did he use some extremely accurate scientific method or experiment to arrive at this date? No, he didn't. Actually, he didn't date the rock at all. He dated the fossil, and he dated the fossil by the chart contained in the invertebrate paleontology text. So the question to ask is, "Where did the author of the paleontology book get this prehistoric date of 640 million years for that specific fossil that dated the rock?" The answer: Darwin's theory. The invertebrate paleontology text, which was written using Darwin's theory, is considered the expert source in dating the fossil. Next, the fossil dates the rock, which is then used to "prove" Darwin's theory true (Morris 13).

Do you see the *circular reasoning* here? Any time you start with a specific theory as being true, and then date an object according to that theory, the date obtained would have to fit into the framework of that theory. There's no other option. You guaranteed the outcome before you ever started by using that specific theory. In other words, the date given to the rock is in no way proof that the theory it was based on is true as some evolutionists like to claim (Morris 13). When speaking of historical science, it is a fallacy to believe that the facts speak for themselves, for they must be interpreted according to a specific framework. The framework behind evolution: naturalism—the assumption that things made themselves. The framework behind creation: There is a God who created the universe as we know it.

Now let's suppose that the rock was organic material instead of sedimentary. How would the professor date a piece of organic material such as hardened lava? In today's laboratory, organic material is dated by measuring the ratios of radioactive isotopes in the rocks. Once known, these ratios can be plugged into a set of mathematical equations which will supposedly give the *absolute age* of that material. The problem is, if you date the organic material with all four of the current methods (uranium-lead method, potassium-argon method, rubidium-strontium model test, samarium-neodymium test), you will likely come back with four extremely different ages. The results of these four tests can vary by hundreds of millions of years. So which of the four ages is dubbed the *absolute age*? It will depend upon where the rock was dug up and what fossils were found nearby. If there are any fossils found near it, once again the invertebrate paleontology book (Darwin's theory) is used to date that fossil. The organic test that fits the closest to the date recorded in the paleontology text is called the *absolute age.* The other three test results are thrown out due to "some kind of unknown contamination."

Dr. John Morris tells the story of once talking with a famous archeologist from the University of Pennsylvania who had discovered an ancient tomb with wooden timbers in the country of Turkey. When Morris asked if he had sent some timber samples off for dating through the carbon-14 method, he was shocked by his reply. The famous archeologist said of course, but then claimed he would "never believe anything that came back from a carbon-14 lab. Nor was he aware of any archeologist in the world who would accept such dates. If the date agreed with what he knew was historically accurate, then the data would be published; if not, it would be ignored. He was obliged to carbon-date artifacts to keep his grant money coming in, and so he always did, but he did not trust the method or its results" (Morris 65).

In both instances, with the sedimentary and organic rock, it was a theory that gave the supposed *absolute age* of the object.

Under normal circumstances, the dating methods proceed as follows (Morris 45):

The scientist will observe the present state of the rock or system which is to be dated.

The scientist will measure the rate of a process presently operating within that system.

The scientist must then **assume** certain things about the past history of the rock or system.

The scientist will calculate how long it would take for that present process, operating throughout the unobserved past, to produce the present state of things in that system.

Let me use an illustration to make this dating process easier to understand. Suppose you're visiting your cousin in the mountains for a few days. Upon arriving at his log cabin, you notice he is preoccupied with cutting firewood. Rather than disturbing him, and since you're wearing good clothes so can't offer to assist, you quietly watch as he works. Out of sheer boredom you begin to count how many pieces of firewood he's able to split and toss onto a nearby stack per minute. For ten straight minutes you count six pieces per minute, meaning one every ten seconds. Is there an **absolute** way to figure out how long your cousin has been cutting wood? If so, how?

The average person would say, "Sure, you can figure out how long he's been cutting by counting the number of pieces piled in the stack and allotting ten seconds per piece. For instance, if there were 120 pieces of wood in the pile, multiply that by 10 seconds and you would get 1200 seconds. Next, since there are 60 seconds per minute, divide the 1200 by 60. The answer would be that he's been cutting wood for twenty minutes." Right or wrong? Wrong! Why? You tell me what is wrong with this conclusion.

Assumptions and Predictions

So what is the problem with saying your cousin has been cutting firewood for twenty minutes? The math worked: 10 seconds x 120 pieces = 1200 seconds ÷ 60 seconds (1 minute) = 20 minutes. The problem: the reason I can't say my conclusion is the "absolute time" is because I began with assumptions. For example, I assumed your cousin had been cutting at the same rate of speed from the moment he first began, neither slowing down nor speeding up the entire time. I assumed there had been no pre-existing firewood in the stack when he first started. I assumed no one had taken any wood from the pile before I arrived. I assumed no one had assisted him in cutting the stack, again before my arrival. So what was the main issue with my conclusion, the reason I cannot refer to it as the "absolute time?" Answer: *I wasn't there at the beginning.* I had to guess the original circumstance, and if my guess was correct, then my conclusion would also have been correct, but if my guess was wrong, my conclusion would likewise have been wrong.

Now consider the biblical story of creation. If you had stood Adam before a panel of scientists five minutes after God created him and asked, "How old is this man?" the panel's response would probably have been, "Well, he's a young man. Our guess is about twenty." In normal circumstances their response would have been correct. Yet their conclusion was very wrong. Why? Because they weren't there at the beginning, and since they weren't there from the beginning they had to make the assumption that this young man standing before them had followed the same growth rate as all humans. They had no way of knowing that the circumstances of his beginning were much different from all other men, that he had been created fully developed.

So the main problem with anyone dating objects or events of "prehistoric history" is *we weren't there.* Therefore, we are forced to make assumptions based on our current knowledge of the world around us. Evolutionists' current "knowledge" is the assumption that Darwin's theory is correct; Christians, on the other hand, make the assumption that God's biblical account of creation is true. So now the question we need to ask is, "Is there a way to tell which of these two accounts is most likely to be accurate?" And the answer to that question is, "Yes, there is." We can examine both of these worldviews, evolution and creation, and then make predictions as to what we should see in our world if each theory is correct. Then the theory whose predictions best fit reality is the theory which is most likely correct.

Take a few minutes to consider the implications of both views—creation and evolution. If evolution is true, what would you expect to find in our world around us? If the biblical account of creation is true, what would you expect to find?

If you were thorough in your examination of these two theories, you would have discovered that what we observe in our world supports God's account of creation and not Darwin's theory of evolution. Let's take a look at what I mean.

Evolution: If evolution were true, we should expect to see transitional forms in nature which are due to an *increase* in genetic information. These transitional creatures would be at various levels of development, with new species coming into existence on a regular basis. Genetically speaking, everything should be getting better and better, not worse and worse. That's not what we see.

Instead of living creatures getting genetically better and better through an increase of genetic information, we see genetic deterioration causing new handicaps and diseases daily.

If evolution were true, we would expect to find transitional forms in the fossil record, connecting one species with its parent species, yet we don't. There is no fossil record of any one species slowly turning into another.

If evolution were true and early man actually began developing around one to three million years ago as "heavy-browed, stooped-shouldered, long-armed knuckle-walkers" (Morris 70), we would expect to see archaeological evidence indicating the existence of these pre-historical apelike man creatures.

If evolution were true and the stone age really lasted 100,000 years prior to modern man and supported a population of between 1 and 10 million individuals, we should find many of the approximately 4 billion bodies that would have been buried in the uppermost soil layer of the earth, yet we find very few. Human bones are very scarce? If man has been around as long as evolution teaches, at the current population growth rate we should have about 10 to the 8600th power (that's 10 with 8600 zeros following it) of people living on planet earth (Miller 70).

Creation: Next, if the biblical story of creation is true we would expect to find intelligent design in nature, an elaborate design that would indicate an awesome God—which is what we see.

We would expect to see separate, distinct kinds of creatures with no transitional forms in existence among either the living or in the fossil records. We would expect to see the extinction of species, not new species coming into existence—which is what we see.

Because of God's curse due to Adam's sin, we would expect to see a tendency for decay in both genetics and nature, with handicaps and diseases increasing on a regular basis. Everything in our world would be running down, not getting better and better—which is what we see.

Since the Bible records the first generation of man to have been abruptly created around 6000 years ago, we would expect to see evidence of modern man quickly springing into existence around that time frame—which is what we see. Our written history even supports this, with an age of about 5000 years.

If the biblical account of creation is true then we must include the destruction of all but Noah and his family (Genesis 6) into our human growth statistics. Given the total number of people on earth today, now approaching 6 billion, and its present growth rate of about 2% per year, it would take only about 1100 years to reach the present population from an original pair (Morris 70). When you include the fact that it wasn't one couple that repopulated the earth, but three couples (Noah's three sons and their wives), and the periods of plagues and wars and violence that wiped out much population, you would expect to see about the same population as is currently present.

If the creation account is true and there was no stone age, considering that humans are soft-body organisms and have a low fossilization potential, we would expect the chances of finding even one human fossil extremely rare—which is what we see.

Conclusion: God's story of creation fits more perfectly with the evidence of our world today.

Teachers: Complete worksheet Chapter 5: Creation versus Evolution—Puzzle 2

Chapter 6: The Bible and Science

Suggested Reading: Chapter 7 in *The Case for a Creator*

Earth: On a Razor's Edge

A thorough reading of chapter 7 of *The Case for a Creator* reveals the uniqueness of our planet when compared to all others in the universe. In short, the new scientific findings of the past fifty years suggest that we are indeed special, even to the point of existing on a *razor's edge*. Our location in the universe, in our galaxy, in our solar system, our size and rotation, composition, structure, atmosphere, temperature, internal dynamics, the mass of the moon and sun, our carbon cycle, oxygen cycle, calcium cycle, nitrogen cycle, phosphorous cycle, sulfur cycle, sodium cycle, and so on—testify to the degree to which our little planet is exquisitely balanced. In fact, they all (along with many other variables) conspire together in an amazing way to enable life to exist on planet earth (Strobel 157). Due to the fine-tuning of our universe, many scientists are now concluding that intelligent life is far rarer than once thought. In fact, evidence indicates that life may very well be unique to planet earth alone (Strobel 189).

Not only is our planet itself unique, but when you compare all life on planet earth, humans are the most important. I realize that many in our humanistic, animal activist society today do not accept this concept but feel that human life is of no greater value than life of any other form. For example, my sister, Patty, owns a veterinary clinic. A few years back she hired a young lady who was an animal activist. This young lady ended up being detrimental to the clinic and my sister because she felt that each animal should be given the same rights (or even superior rights) as a human. Here's an example of what I mean: One day a pit bull they were trying to muzzle in order to treat attacked my sister, and of course she defended herself in the manner they are taught by bringing her knee up and blocking his path to her throat and face. When he repeated the attack, she once again thrust her knee into his face to protect herself. Finally, when the dog attacked a third time and she was unable to defend herself, her husband, the veterinarian, kicked the dog away when he was within inches of his target—her throat! This temporarily stunned the dog, enabling them to finally muzzle him. This young animal activist saw the entire scene and protested that she believed it was animal abuse. In her mind, it was wrong to hurt the dog in order to prevent him from tearing Patty's throat and face apart. Finally, when Patty had come to her wits end with this employee, she asked her this question, "If there was a semi roaring down the road and my son and his dog were in its path, supposing you had time to save only one of the two, which would you choose?" Her reply was, "Well, I couldn't make that decision. It would be wrong to choose one life over the other." To which Patty responded, "I could. I would save my son." Needless to say, this employee only lasted three days before she was given her *pink slip*.

This notion that other forms of life are of equal value to human life is utterly rejected by Christianity. "The Bible teaches that human life is not only the most valuable life on earth, but that it is infinitely more valuable than any other form of earthly life. Not all the rainforests, not all the seal pups, not all the great whales, equal the value of one human soul. This truth might seem outrageous when you compare the value of the whales against the value of a person whom you do not like or know. But it becomes rather wonderful if you compare it with the value either of your own life or of the life of someone you love. How wonderful it is to know that the God who made all things, loves and values you above all things" (Lansdown 26-29)!

The Bible itself testifies to our special place in God's creation. Consider this: there are two chapters (Genesis 1 & 2) that give the account of the creation of our little solar system, the earth and all of its contents, man, and God's relationship with man. Yet for all of the rest of creation outside of our little solar system, all the other massive solar systems and galaxies in existence, God attributes only five words, "He made the stars also" (Genesis 1:16). Contrary to what Hollywood science fiction movies teach, planet earth has the preeminence among the planets.

Also, the key theme woven throughout the entire sixty-six books of the Bible can be summed up in three very important words, God's Redemptive Plan, and this redemptive plan isn't for seals, dogs, or animals of any kind, it is for humans alone. So from Genesis 1:1 to Revelation 22:21 the creation of man, the fall of man, and the salvation of man has the center of God's attention. Think of the implications of this! The entire Bible deals with the creation of man's world and man himself, yet again, only five small words cover the creation of the entire rest of the universe. This clearly indicates that humans are the most important of God's worldly creation!

Yes, man is special, and the Bible teaches that God created man with purpose. Genesis 1:27-28 reads, "So God created man in his own image, in the image of God He created him; male and female He created them. God blessed them and said to them, 'Be fruitful and increase in number; fill the earth and subdue it. Rule over the fish of the sea and the birds of the air and over every living creature that moves on the ground.'"

Even science is beginning to verify at least one of the purposes for which man was created. Let me repeat a few points from your reading in Lee Strobel's book, *The Case for a Creator*.

> "And rather than our lives being purposeless, scientists for the first time are uncovering concrete evidence that suggests at least one surprising purpose for which we are created—that is, to discover and learn about the surroundings in which we have been placed" (Strobel 156).

> For example, the same conditions that give us a habitable planet also make our location perfect for scientific measurement and discovery (Strobel 186). Out of the "nine planets with their more than sixty-three moons in our solar system, the Earth's surface is the best place where observers can witness a total solar eclipse" (Strobel 185).

> Jay Wesley Richards stated that "there is no obvious reason to assume that the very same rare properties that allow for our existence would also provide the best overall setting to make discoveries about the world around us. In fact, we believe that the conditions for making scientific discoveries on Earth are so fine-tuned that you would need a great amount of faith to attribute them to mere chance" (Strobel 187).

Science Taught in God's Word?

God does not want his creation, man, whom He has given a place of preeminence, to be ignorant of his plan and purpose here on earth. That's why He has given us His word, the God-breathed, inerrant, Holy Scriptures. One of the proofs that our Bible is the authentic word of God is the many scientific statements that were recorded within its pages long before our world was aware of their truthfulness. Only a God who created could have knowledge of these characteristics of His universe thousands of years prior to man discovering them. Go to www.Biblegateway.com and look up the following phrases. You may have to search through several verses before you locate the correct one, but once you do, copy its reference and the verse onto this worksheet next to the corresponding phrase. I used the *New Living Translation* in preparing this worksheet, so it will make your work easier if you use it as well. Once you have copied these references and verses, write a simple summary of the scientific principle taught in that specific reference.

. . . like the stars of the sky . . .—

. . . even the stars differ . . .—

. . . sky over empty space . . .—

. . . winds blow north and south . . .—

. . . life of any creature is in the blood . . .—

. . . plants and trees from the dust of the ground . . .—

. . . makes for good health . . .—

. . . cheerful heart is good medicine . . .—

. . . draws up the water vapor . . .—

. . . rain in his thick clouds . . .—

. . . waters return again to the rivers . . .—

. . . the circle of the earth . . .—

. . . long before the world began . . .—

. . . not come from anything that was seen . . .—

. . . stretch out the starry curtain . . .—

. . . wear out like old clothing . . .—

. . . hangs the earth on nothing . . .—

. . . Pleiades or Orion . . .—

. . . laws of the universe . . .—

. . . water that covered even the mountains . . .—

. . . springs from which the seas come . . .—

. . . swims in the ocean currents . . . —

. . . heavens cannot be measured . . . —

. . . made two great lights . . . —

Witnessing to an Evolutionist

Now that we've studied the uniqueness of planet earth, write one paragraph over the following topics:

Why did God make such a vast universe if we are the only privileged planet?

God has obviously given us a place of privilege in His heart. This is evidenced by the fact that He sent His Son to die on the cross to pay the price for our sins so we could be reunited with Him in eternity. Matthew 28:19 reads, "Go therefore and make disciples of all the nations, baptizing them in the name of the Father and the Son and the Holy Spirit" (NKJV). In Luke 14:23 we read, "Go out into the highways and hedges, and compel them to come in, that my house may be filled" (NKJV). God's desire is for us to witness to a lost and dying world in order to reach as many people as possible with His word. I want you to think back over the material we've covered so far in this course. Suppose you had a friend who didn't believe in God because of his belief in evolution. How could you use what you've learned so far as a tool to witness to this friend? Write a paragraph explaining how your newly obtained knowledge could be of assistance in your witness to this friend.

Teachers: Complete worksheet Chapter 6: Mid-way Opportunity

Chapter 7: Physical Evidences

The *Limiting Age Factor*

As we studied in topic three, the formation of the earth doesn't fit into operational science. It is an event from the past that cannot be repeated in a laboratory and is not occurring in nature today. Therefore, scientists must make assumptions that seem reasonable based on collected observable data. While evolutionists and "old earth" thinkers interpret the data in a way that supports their theory, "young earth" advocates interpret it entirely different and therefore arrive at a totally different conclusion. So which view is correct? What we need to know is, "Is it possible to eliminate one of the two views by using scientific data?" And the answer is, "Yes, it is." No, we can't prove the age of the earth through this observable data, but we can certainly limit its age by using what is known as the *Limiting Age Factor*. So our question to answer is, "Are there any factors about the earth that limit its age?"

Here's an illustration showing what is meant by the limiting age factor. Suppose a sunken ship is discovered off the coast of Florida. As the divers are examining this vessel, they find a treasure chest locked inside one of the ship's many rooms. When this treasure chest is brought to the surface for further examination, they discover a small jewelry box among its contents. While most of the contents of this chest date back to about 1000 A.D., inside this jewelry box they discover a golden coin with an engraved date of 1780. Even though the rest of the contents of the treasure chest might seem to point to the ship sinking somewhere around the turn of the millennium, this golden coin seriously limits that date. With the discovery of this coin, it is evident that this ship was still above the surface of the water in the year 1780, since they didn't mint 1780 coins before the year 1780. Therefore, we can safely date the sinking of this specific vessel sometime during or after the year 1780. The coin became the *limiting age factor*.

How does this limiting age factor relate to the age of the earth? If there is any evidence that limits the age of the earth, then the earth cannot be any older than that specific evidence. I'm going to give you some evidence to look up that does indeed limit the age of the earth, but before I do I want you to be aware of the fact that evolutionists do attempt to reconcile a ***few*** of these limiting dates into their billions of years theory, but they are only able to accomplish this by making a series of ***improbable and unproven assumptions*** (Humphreys 1). Young earth creationists, on the other hand, don't have to make any assumptions or revisions to the biblical timeframe of creation because it fits perfectly within the frame of this scientific data.

Research the following *Limiting Age Factors* and identify the limiting age of each specific factor. Include a description of each factor and underline the limiting age indicator. I have finished the first one as an example for you. Some will take a little more effort to search for, but many will be found on the following site: www.answersingenesis.org/docs/4005.asp?vPrint=1. (Teachers please do the following research. For those of you who are not earning CEU's, I have the answers to this section listed at the end of this course for everyone else.)

Too little sediment of all kinds in earth's crust: The time needed to accumulate the entire sedimentary crust on the earth's surface is only 1.25 billion years, far too few for the theory of evolution (Morris 88).

Galaxies wind themselves up too fast:

Earth's rotation slowing down:

Moon is moving away from the earth at 2 to 3 inches per year:

Not enough salt in the sea:

Continents would have been flattened by erosion:

Not enough mud on the sea floor:

Comets disintegrate too quickly:

Earth's magnetic field decays too fast:

Biological material decays too fast:

Underground oil deposits are under too much pressure:

Jupiter, Saturn, Uranus, Neptune, and Pluto are cooling off:

Too few supernova remnants:

Too much helium in minerals:

Too little moon dust:

Written history is too short:

Too much carbon 14 in deep geologic strata:

Not enough Stone Age skeletons:

Many strata are too tightly bent:

Fossil radioactivity shortens geologic "ages" to a few years:

The Breathtaking Grand Canyon!

Old earth theories teach that the rock layers of the Grand Canyon were laid down a particle at a time over hundreds of millions of years, and that the great canyon was later gradually carved out by the Colorado River over the past two million years. If this is true then the biblical story of creation—which we have already seen dates to about 6000 years ago—is impossible. But does this gradual carving out of the Grand Canyon by the Colorado River theory really fit the evidence? Let's briefly examine this theory, as well as the more recent biblical creationist theory that not only fits the geological evidence but the biblical timeframe as well. After all, if it did take millions of years to form the Grand Canyon, then the biblical story of creation is in error.

Again, remember that any time you study events of the past you're in the realm of historical science not operational science, which means assumptions must be made, and if you're beginning assumptions are wrong, your conclusion will be wrong as well. Having said this, it is significant to note that the formation of this great canyon may not completely fit into the category of historical science. Why? Because the native Havasupai Indians, whose ancestors lived in this remote canyon for centuries before white settlers arrived, passed down from one generation to the next eyewitness accounts of a time (approximately 1000 years ago) when mighty flood waters scalped out the great canyon. These eyewitness accounts, if they are true, place the formation of the canyon into the category of operational science because it was witnessed by one or more of their five senses. But for argument sake, let's pretend that these eyewitness accounts are not true and study the canyon's formation solely based on historical science.

First of all, the traditional theory that the rock layers were laid down over hundreds of millions of years doesn't fit the evidence. Mike Oard, M.S. Atmospheric Science, writes that, "Recently dated sedimentary rocks just west of the Grand Canyon have forced some evolutionary scientists to postulate that the Canyon formed quickly sometime between one and six million years ago. If the Canyon formed rapidly, processes observed today, such as gully-washing thunderstorms, seem less likely to have played a major role in carving the Grand Canyon and its side canyons. A catastrophic mechanism for the formation of the Grand Canyon seems more likely, even within the evolutionary model. Within the creation framework, the Grand Canyon originated only several thousand years ago as a direct or indirect result of Noah's flood. So we would expect that thunderstorms and flash floods would have had no effect on the Canyon's original formation" (Vail 66).

Tom Vail has written a book that is a collection of writings by some very qualified scientists and theologians explaining this new Grand Canyon formation theory. If there's any way you can get your hands on this book titled, *Grand Canyon: A Different View,* it would certainly be worth your read. The scientists in Tom Vail's book examine the evidence found in the canyon and present the case that the canyon itself wasn't the result of a "little water (Colorado River) over a huge amount of time, but a huge amount of water over a little amount of time." This is a new and growing view among many geologists today who, as a result of the eruption of Mt. Saint Helens and other similar current events, are now realizing the scalping power involved in catastrophic events.

Gary Parker, Ed.D. Biology, points out another very serious problem concerning the traditional view that has been taught for decades—that a little water over a huge amount of time formed the canyon. Dr. Parker writes, "One thing is sure: The Colorado River did not do it. The river starts about 12,000 feet up in the Rocky Mountains of western Colorado. By the time it gets to the head of the Grand Canyon, it's at an elevation of only 3,000 feet or so. And that is the problem. The Grand Canyon is definitely not a lowland valley. The North Rim of the Canyon is over 8,000 feet high! For the Colorado River to carve the Canyon, it would first have had to have hacked its way almost a mile uphill! Water just doesn't do that, especially when there is the means to flow downhill in a different direction" (Vail 62).

With the Colorado River formation of the canyon disqualified, is there any evidence that the canyon might have been formed by a huge amount of water over a small amount of time? Yes, there is. Just above the canyon on the surface of the Colorado Plateau, geologists have observed a saucer shaped basin that appears to have once been a series of huge connecting lakes—30,000 square miles of lakes, which is enough water to fill Lake Michigan three times over. This series of lakes might well have been formed by the catastrophic flood waters of Noah's day. Steve Austin, Pd.D. Geology, believes that the weight of evidence favors the theory that the Grand Canyon was formed by a breaching event—probably the failure of a natural dam formed by the Kaibab Upwarp (Austin 94). The fact that the beginning of the Grand Canyon is at the same spot where this breach appears is pretty good evidence that it was formed by the raging waters that passed through this breach.

If you live in a location where you can do a small experiment, I want you to try something. Some time when you're outside, go over and turn on your outdoor water faucet. Put your thumb on the end of the hose and force the water to spray like a power washer. Next, place the end of the hose (still spraying like a power washer) about an inch from the ground. What do you suppose will happen? Regardless of whether or not you try this experiment, you know exactly what would happen. The pressure from the spraying water would dig a hole in the ground. The more water and pressure, the bigger the hole you carve. Now, try and imagine the amount of water that it would take to fill Lake Michigan three times over power spraying a hole into the ground. I certainly have no problem imagining a mighty canyon being formed by 30,000 square miles of raging water.

Another piece of evidence supporting this new argument is located just outside the city of San Diego. Think about it for just a moment. If a catastrophic event did rapidly carve the canyon, wouldn't you expect to find the mud and boulder contents that washed out of that canyon somewhere at the canyon's end. Of course you would. And that's exactly what we find just outside the city of San Diego. Interestingly enough, this strangely placed pile of dirt and rock isn't a mineral match to the San Diego area, yet it perfectly matches that of the canyon.

Do an online search of both www.nwcreation.net/mtsthelens.html and www.creationwiki.org/Rapid erosion on Mt. St. Helens shows Grand Canyon could form suddenly and read the information given. After reading these articles over the eruption of Mt. Saint Helens, consider how this modern day eruption helps to validate the biblical creationist viewpoint that the Grand Canyon was the result of a sudden catastrophic event and not created over hundreds of millions of years.

Food For Thought: When you visited the Grand Canyon or watched a documentary about its origin, were you given both sides of the story—that the canyon was either formed by a little water (flowing uphill over a mile) over a huge amount of time or a huge amount of water (flowing downhill as water naturally runs) over a small amount of time? If not, why do you think evolutionists try so desperately hard to prevent any view except their own from being presented?

Noah's Catastrophic Flood

In topic two, you looked up some Bible verses dealing with the creation of the world. One of these verses was 2 Peter 3:3-6, "First, I want to remind you that in the last days there will be scoffers who will laugh at the truth and do every evil thing they desire. This will be their argument: 'Jesus promised to come back, did he? Then where is he? Why, as far back as anyone can remember everything has remained exactly the same.' They deliberately forget that God made the heavens by the word of his command, and he brought the earth up from the water and surrounded it with water. Then he used the water to destroy the world with a mighty flood" (NLT). Not only do these verses make reference to man intentionally denying special creation by the spoken Word of God, they also speak of his willful denial of Noah's global flood. But why? Why would man feel the need to deny there once having been a global flood? I can easily understand why he would deny special creation, because if, "In the beginning God didn't create," then he would be free to live his life the way he pleased. But if, "In the beginning God did create," it means that man will one day be held accountable to that Creator for how he lives his life, and for a man who wants to live his life his own way, that's a scary proposition.

But why would rebellious man also feel the need to deny the story of Noah's deluge? Why would it matter whether or not there was once a global catastrophic flood that destroyed the whole face of the earth? Really, the answer is quite simple. If such an awesome catastrophic event is history, then billions of plants and animals would have been rapidly and randomly buried with water, mud, and pressure, immediately beneath the earth's surface, causing billions and billions of fossils mixed without order or cause. And that's the problem. If a global flood did produce the enormous amounts of randomly placed fossils present today, then Darwin's theory of millions of years didn't. Also, Darwin taught that the oldest of all living creatures would be fossilized in the lowest levels of the earth; while the newest and most recent of creatures would appear in the upper most levels. But what do we find beneath the earth's surface? Remember the Cambrian Explosion? The reason it counters Darwin's theory is because it reveals billions of creatures fossilized in a *random and confusing manner*, just as you would expect had they been caused by a global flood. Thus the Cambrian Explosion literally turns Darwin's tree of life upside-down, yet amazingly enough it fits perfectly with the evidence of there once having been a great catastrophic flood.

Yet even more amazing is that many well thought of theologians have ignored these evidences of the great flood and developed their own theories, theories that fit Darwin's theory of evolution. Two of the most common of these theories presented are (1) that it was only a local flood but seemed global to Noah and his family because all they could see was water, and (2) that it was a tranquil event, not the earth shattering, continent-moving, raging torrent that the Bible describes.

Before I speak on these local and tranquil theories, I want you to stop and read Genesis 6-9. Think about these two proposed theories as you read. When you are finished reading list as many biblical problems with these theories as you can.

Key Evidences of a Global Flood

Biblically speaking, here is a list of some evidence that it was a global flood and not local.

The water remained for over a year.

The water was approximately 22 feet above the highest mountaintops for nine months. That would have been impossible had it been merely a local flood.

The rainbow appeared for the first time after Noah and his family left the ark, indicating a radical change in atmospheric conditions.

The purpose of the flood was to destroy all human life upon planet earth because of man's wickedness.

The purpose of the ark was to "keep seed alive upon the face of the earth." This purpose would have been unnecessary had it been only a local flood.

Why would God instruct Noah to build an ark that would take 120 years, when moving his family away from that local area would have been sufficient to save them?

Why would God have Noah take animals aboard the ark if they, too, could have simply migrated a few hundred miles away

God said it was global—"destroy all life upon the earth," not "partial life in a local region."

Historically Speaking, here is some evidence that a global flood once occurred?

There are at least 272 stories from every culture around the world that speak of a global flood, and although the details often vary, these stories always refer to a man named Noah (or similar name) who was saved from the flood to repopulate the earth. If it were a local or "calm" event, its occurrence would have faded away into history without much notice. Instead, these stories have been passed down as actual history for millennium.

The flood account is found on Babylonian, Acadian, and Samarian tablets now housed in the British museum. These tablets date back to 700 B.C.

We have some ancient Chinese accounts that date back even further than the tablets in the British museum.

In the mid 1800's, George Smith began piecing together some 25,000 pieces of clay tablets unearthed in the city of Nineveh dating back to the 6th century B.C. In 1872 Smith came upon the account of an ancient ship paralleling the biblical account of Noah's Ark. These tablets became known as the Gilgamesh Tablets.

There have been over 100 sightings of Noah's art on Mt. Ararat dating from the 5th century B.C. to 1990 A.D. These sightings include such historians and explorers as Josephus, Eusebius, Marco Polo, and a good number of U.S. military personal. B.J. Corbin's book titled *The Explorers of Ararat* record and detail these sightings.

The genealogical records of many European kings can be traced back to Japheth, one of Noah's three sons.

Analysis of population growth confirms a zero population at the estimated time of the flood.

Civilization seems to have originated in the Ararat/Babylon region, exactly where the Bible story places Noah and his family when they left the ark.

The Ice Age started very quickly, and this would have required a cataclysmic event such as a global flood to trigger such a rapid climatic change. A slow, gradual decrease in temperature as evolutionists teach would have produced a very cold earth, but not an icy earth.

Fossil graveyards are found worldwide, and in rocks of all ages. Only a catastrophic global flood could have achieved this.

Marine fossils can be found on the crests of mountains alongside land animals.

Vast quantities of fossiliferous rock indicate there was once a global flood.

The sudden dying out of dinosaurs and other prehistoric creatures.

Scientifically Speaking, "We see over 22 unique features on our planet which can now be systematically explained as the result of a cataclysmic global flood whose waters erupted from subterranean chambers (Genesis 7:11) with an energy release exceeding the explosion of 10,000,000,000 hydrogen bombs. Some of these features include the mid-oceanic ridge, the continental shelves and slopes, the ocean trenches and rings of fire, the oil and coal deposits, the Ice Age, herds of frozen Mammoths (result of sudden ice age), the major mountain ranges paralleling oceanic ridges, strata and layered fossil, earthquakes, magnetic variations on the ocean floor, submarine canyons, methane hydrates, over thrusts, volcanoes and lava, geothermal heat, limestone, metamorphic rock, plateaus, the Moho, salt domes, changing axis tilt, and the jigsaw puzzle fit of the continents." This statement was recorded in a video (*Encounters with the Unexplained* produced by Grizzly Adams Productions Inc.) by a scientist working for a government scientific organization back when government employees were still allowed to make such statements without fear of retribution.

Biblical Questions Concerning Noah's Ark

How could all of those animals fit on one ship?

Answer: The biblical dimensions of the ark make it longer than a football field and taller than a four story building. To be exact, it would have been 450' long, 75' wide and 45' tall. When you consider the enormous storing capability of such a great vessel (520 railroad boxcars filled with 40,000,000 tons of cargo), you should have no problem believing that it could have contained two of each unclean kind of animal (Genesis 6:20) and seven of each clean (Genesis 7:2) kind (Morris 14). All modern types of animals could have come from about 5,000 kinds or less, and with this vessel being big enough to haul more than 50,000 animals the average size of a sheep, it was plenty large enough to perform its purpose (Video: *Noah's Ark on Ararat: Encounters with the Unexplained*).

How could all of the many kinds of dinosaurs fit on the ark?

Answer: Creation scientists have narrowed down the *kinds* of dinosaurs to about 50—that's after eliminating the dinosaurs that appear to be the same but have been given different names by different cultures, thus making their numbers seem much more numerous than actual evidence indicates. Since dinosaurs were reptilian creatures, meaning they grew larger with age, it wouldn't have been necessary to use up that much space aboard the ark to save two of each kind. Also, remember that God's purpose was to save these animals from extinction so they could repopulate the earth once they left the ark. Why would He have chosen a great-great-great-great-great grandma and grandpa dinosaur, the largest of their kind, to bring aboard the ark? They would have had far fewer years to bare offspring than two young adult dinosaurs whose size was probably no larger than that of an elephant. If you take all 50 kinds of dinosaurs, some being as small as a chicken, and average their sizes together, you will discover the average size was that of a sheep. Double that number for a male and female, and the dinosaurs would have taken the same amount of space as 100 sheep.

Wouldn't Noah's ark have sunk in the raging flood waters?

Answer: Remember that Noah's ark wasn't designed to move from one location to another as a normal ship. Its purpose was to be nothing more than a floating warehouse. Studies have shown that Noah's ark could have been tilted up to a 90 degree angle and still righted itself in the waters. As a matter of fact, many of today's ships are built with similar dimensions to that of the ark because of its amazing sea worthiness (Video: *Noah's Ark on Ararat: Encounters with the Unexplained*).

If Noah took dinosaurs aboard the ark, then man and dinosaurs lived at the same time. Is there any evidence that this is true? After all, evolution teaches that dinosaurs died out over 65,000,000 years before man even came onto the scene.

Answer: Yes, there is plenty of evidence of man and dinosaurs (often called dragons) lived at the same time. Legends are often based on fact, even though some details are embellished through the ages, and there are plenty of legends of man's encounter with dinosaurs. In Paul S. Taylor's book, *The Great Dinosaur Mystery and the Bible,* he discusses many of these legends which originated from various cultures. These stories are recorded in ancient literature from "Africa, India, Europe, the Middle East, the Orient, and every other part of the world" (Taylor 36). Specific locations include Babylon, Scandinavia, France, Europe, Italy, China, Ireland (900 A.D.), Africa, and Arabia (460 B.C.). Many ancient cave drawings, pictures and carvings on pottery also expose mans' past connection with the dinosaur.

If man and dinosaurs lived at the same time, why doesn't the Bible mention them?

Answer: It does! In Job 40 and 41 we see animals mentioned whose descriptions fit only into the dinosaur category. "The Bible uses ancient names like 'behemoth' and 'tannin.' Behemoth means kingly, gigantic beasts. Tannin is a term which includes dragon-like animals and great sea creatures such as whales, giant squids, and marine reptiles like the plesiosaurs that may have become extinct" (Taylor 18). The Bible describes behemoth as being so huge that he didn't need to fear anything, and his tail was so long and strong that God compared it to a cedar tree—one of the largest and most spectacular trees of the ancient world (Taylor 19). Today, some people have mistakenly guessed the behemoth to be an elephant or hippopotamus, but have you ever seen an elephant or hippo's tail? They look more like a pencil than a huge and strong cedar. If you look up Job 40 in your Bible, you might well find the words elephant or hippopotamus inserted into these scriptures, but this is man's insertion and not what was originally written.

Also, in Job 41 you will find the description of a great sea creature, a creature who man would never even attempt to capture. God stated that "nothing on earth is his equal—a creature without fear" (Job 41:33, NIV). Leviathan's size was enormous, his jaws were strong, his teeth were great, and he was an awesome swimmer. In Job 41, God asks the questions, "Can you draw out Leviathan with a hook, or snare his tongue with a line which you lower? Can you put a reed through his nose, or pierce his jaw with a hook? . . . Can you fill his skin with harpoons, or his head with fishing spears" (NKJV)? Then He gives the further description of this great creature by saying, " . . . indeed, any hope of overcoming him is false . . . no one is so fierce that he would dare stir him up . . . Though the sword reaches him, it cannot avail; Nor does spear, dart, or javelin. He regards iron as straw, and bronze as rotten wood. The arrow cannot make him flee; . . . He laughs at the threat of javelins" (NKJV). This description causes many scientists to believe that Leviathan might have been a Kronosaurus. As far as we know, he was the fiercest and most overwhelming animal to ever swim the seas (Taylor 46). Living in the oceans, these animals may or may not be extinct. Examine the following report: "A creature very much like these was reported during World War I by a German submarine. Captain Georg von Forstner described what happened: 'On July 30, 1915, our U28 torpedoed the British steamer *Iberian* carrying a rich cargo in the North Atlantic. The steamer sank quickly, the bow sticking almost vertically into the air. When it had gone for about twenty-five seconds there was a violent explosion. A little later pieces of wreckage, and among them a gigantic sea animal (writhing and struggling wildly), was shot out of the water to a height of 60 to 100 feet. At that moment I had with me in the conning tower my officers of the watch, the chief engineer, the navigator, and the helmsman. Simultaneously we all drew one another's attention to this wonder of the seas . . . we were unable to identify it. We did not have the time to take a photograph, for the animal sank out of sight after ten or fifteen seconds. It was about 60-feet long, was like a crocodile in shape and had four limbs with powerful webbed feet and a long tail tapering to a point.'"

Again, some Bible translators have wrongly identified this animal as an alligator, as some of your Bibles will testify. Yet God clearly states that no man would even dare try to overcome him, let alone wrestle with him. There's no way this awesome creature is an alligator. Gracious! We've got men who wrestle and defeat alligators! How frustrating it is when people, even if their intentions are good, take away from the inspiration of God's Word by inserting in their own ideas. And these verses do validate the inspiration of the Bible, for it speaks of creatures unknown to modern man for hundreds of years.

What happened to all the dinosaurs?

Answer: After the flood the earth was a very different place. Most of the world was left covered with water, and the ice age, earthquakes, and volcanoes continued to plague the planet on a grand scale. Temperatures had become extreme. Some parts of the world became much hotter, which eventually led to the great deserts. In other places, snow began to fall because of the freezing cold, producing a short ice age—which would have been the natural result of a global flood. In Genesis 2:5 we discover rain was originally not necessary because the dew of the night was sufficient to water the earth. This would be similar to a terrarium, and the only way we know this could have been scientifically possible was if God had surrounded the earth with a great protective canopy. This great canopy would have been destroyed by the "fountains of the deep" blowing into the sky with astounding force, resulting in harmful radiation from the sun hitting the earth in much larger doses than ever before. After this, many parts of the world became too harsh for dinosaurs to survive, and no longer did the earth have the same great forests of huge, nutritious plants necessary to keep such monstrous beasts alive. As the remaining dinosaurs grew larger and larger, it would have been hard for them to locate enough food to survive. But it wasn't just the dinosaurs that died off. Great numbers of creatures have become extinct in the thousands of years since the flood. As a matter of fact, in the last 350 years alone almost 400 species have disappeared. Today, some experts claim that one or more species of plants and animals may be lost every day (Taylor 34-35).

Where did all the dinosaur fossils come from?

In the past half century numerous dinosaur graveyards have been discovered, some containing tens of thousands of skeletal remains. This indeed raises the question of what could possibly have happened to cause all of these—sometimes enormously huge creatures—to all die out and then fossilize. Suggestions such as meteorites, volcanoes, disease, local floods, and even constipation have been offered to answer this question; but these suggestions only pose a greater problem. If an animal dies under normal circumstances its remains are eaten by other animals and insects and within a few weeks there is often no evidence that the animal ever existed. In some cases the skeletal remains might remain a bit longer, yet eventually it does decay and turn to dust. What then could have caused millions of dinosaurs all over the world to die off around the same time and in a means conducive to causing their skeletons to turn to fossils?

While digging up and studying these remains much evidence has been found to indicate that these great animals were buried alive by rapidly flowing flood waters. Sound familiar? It should. Since dinosaurs were land animals they were created on the sixth day of creation with all of the rest of the land animals, so all but two of each kind would have perished during the great deluge. It's interesting to note that many evolutionists try to explain these large dinosaur graveyards as having been created by a flood, although they are always quick to include qualifying words such as seasonal, flash, or regional, lest their readers mistakenly assume they believe in the great deluge of Noah's day. Can you imagine a flash flood being so strong that it could bury thousands of enormously huge dinosaurs? That doesn't even make sense.

The common thread between all of these massive dinosaur graveyards is the evidence that they could have been—and some certainly were—the result of a catastrophic flood such as the one described in the Bible. For instance, probably the largest bone-bed in the world is located in Montana where it is estimated that 10,000 duckbill dinosaurs are entombed. Their bones are disjointed, severed, and even split lengthwise, and they are positioned from the east to the west. Many are standing upright, indicating they were involved in some type of debris flow. No mud slide or mere local flood could have produced enough force to take these two to three-ton animals and smash them around with so much force that their bones—still embedded in their flesh—split lengthwise. It's also interesting to note that no baby dinosaurs or young juveniles have been found. If these enormous creatures demise was due to a catastrophic global flood, their young would not have been able to keep up with them as they fled to higher ground. Therefore, you would expect to find exactly what has been found, no young juveniles or babies among these burial grounds (www.answersingenesis.org/tj/v11/i2/dinosaur.asp.)

Could a global flood like that of Noah's day actually bury these enormous creatures this quickly? Absolutely! "Catastrophic burial in sandy flood sediment can be so immediate that an animal could be completely immobilized and buried before it had much chance to react" (www.answersingenesis.org/articles/am/v1/n1/two-fighting-dinosaurs). We have discovered a female Ichthyosaur dinosaur fossilized in the very act of giving birth, and two other dinosaurs, a Velociraptor and Protoceratops, buried in a manner that appears they were fighting. They may have actually been fighting when they were buried, or the flood waters may have placed them into those positions so that it merely appears they were.

Doesn't it take millions of years for fossils to form?

Evolutionists teach that it takes thousands, even millions of years for a rock or fossil to form, thus they date the millions of fossilized skeletal remains to be millions of years old. Yet more recently evidence has been discovered that proves it doesn't take an enormous amount of time for fossils to form, just the right conditions. One example: a miner's hat was found in a mine in Tasmania where it had been covered with mineral water for fifty years. This hat had turned to solid rock merely by sitting in the right chemical water solution for only fifty years, far short of evolutionist's required millions of years (www.answersingenesis.org/creation/v17/i3/fossil_hat.asp).

Interesting facts about T-Rex and Brontosaurs.

Tyrannosaurus Rex, with his sharp teeth and claws is pictured by Hollywood as a great, fierce, man and dinosaur eating monster. Yet is this depiction actually accurate? Current research suggests that T-Rex would not have been able to move very quickly, so most other dinosaurs could probably have easily escaped. Also, fossil evidence indicates that T-Rex walked in a stooped-over position and probably waddled like a duck. Next, his teeth were not rooted very well (about 1 inch of root system) meaning, in a fierce battle the first vicious bite he took of his opponent would probably have pulled every tooth he had straight out of his mouth. Lastly, the food remnants found in his fossilized stomach and manure are mostly plants and trees, not meat. In other words, he was apparently more of a scavenger than a true hunter.

Brontosaurus, the hero of many Hollywood movies, who has been pictured in every dinosaur book and museum for the last hundred years, is a totally fictitious dinosaur. Let me explain what I mean by this. The skeletal body of Brontosaurus was discovered with the head missing, so to complete the skeleton, the scientist added a skull that was found three or four miles away. For many years no one knew this! Eventually it was discovered that Brontosaurus' skeleton actually belonged to a type of Diplodocus, and his skull was from an Apatosaurus. So regretfully, Disney's *Little Foot,* never really existed.

With the Garden of Eden being destroyed by the flood, is there any way of knowing where it was originally located?

Answer: Absolutely not! I have heard many claims of how the Garden of Eden was originally located in Iraq, but this is absurd. There is no way we can know this. Noah's flood was a global, earth-shattering deluge. It was enormous enough to break apart continents and drastically reform landscaping. The ark floated above the mutilating power of these flood waters for over a year before coming to rest on the highest mountain peak available. When the waters receded, there was no way of telling where man's original civilizations had once been located. Yes, there are two rivers in Iraq that carry the same names as the rivers mentioned before the flood, but this proves nothing. Man has often named new places/rivers/cities in honor of old ones. Because the Euphrates and Tigris are pinpointed in Iraq today does not mean they were the original rivers present at the time of the creation of the earth.

You might also enjoy checking out the dinosaur tracks and human footprints found together in Glen Rose, Texas. The human print walks right through the dinosaur track and both are fossilized together. The only way this is possible is if the mud was still wet when both walked through.

Chapter 8: Wishful Thinking

Suggested Reading: Chapter 8 & 9 in *The Case for a Creator*

Darwin's Black Box

With the release of movies like *Raiders of the Lost Ark,* most Americans are now fully aware of the historical science of archeology. What is archeology? It's the hunt for and study of ancient cultures. So like Indiana Jones, the hero of *Raiders of the Lost Ark,* an archeologist's job is to carefully dig up relics and clues of the past in an attempt to reconstruct how ancient people lived. Although most Americans know what archeology is, many are unaware of what pushed this historical science to the forefront of this modern era. You see, archeology has been around for centuries, but it didn't become a serious science until the 19th century, and regretfully, its main stimulant was to discover evidence in support of Darwin's theory. Unfortunately, as time passed many archeologists began to accept the idea of evolution as fact rather than a theory needing to be proven, and even today many archeologists set out with the specific purpose of finding support for the theory of evolution in the relics of man's past. The result of their biased purpose is the many one-sided, questionable and even fanciful interpretations of relics discovered (Combee 52).

Although archeology was thrust to the forefront with the purpose of proving Darwin's theory true, many of its findings actually call the theory into question. You see, rather than digging up the missing link, one by one many of the biblical critics' *supposed errors and myths in the Bible* are being eliminated; and rather than discovering a primitive and crude thick-browed, stooped over, half human ancestor, it has shown our ancestors to have been extremely intelligent and inventive—which is contrary to evolution but exactly what the Bible teaches.

Darwin believed that with time archeological discoveries would validate his theory with evidence of the slow progression from one kind to another. But again, the exact opposite has happened. Instead of finding links between known organisms as Darwin's tree of origin pictures, it has been discovered—through lack of evidence—that these links are mostly imaginary. This has proven to be a major obstacle with Darwinism (Patterson 38). How did Darwin explain this progression from one kind to another? He believed, as most all scientists of his day, that the cell was the simplest unit on the planet. It looked like a tiny glob of Jello with a dark spot as the nucleus. It could do interesting things like divide and move around, but they didn't know how it did them. It was Darwin's "Black Box"—a term scientists use when describing a system or machine they find interesting but don't know how to explain (Strobel 196).

Before I continue, I want to remind you that evolution has been divided into two different categories: microevolution and macroevolution. Evolutionists often misrepresent the creationist point of view by claiming that we don't believe in either, thus attempting to make us look ignorant and unlearned. This could not be farther from the truth. As a matter of fact, the Bible actually teaches microevolution, which is nothing more than variation within a species. What it doesn't teach and what we don't believe is macroevolution, or large-scale, beneficial mutations which require huge amounts of added genetic information and change one species into another. These large-scale, beneficial mutations are what geneticist John F. McDonald has called the "great Darwinian paradox," because they don't occur within nature. On the contrary, within nature, natural selection has only been shown to change organisms within the boundaries of that specific biblical kind.

So what exactly is a biblical *kind*? The biblical *kind* is usually a broader category than our modern term *species.* For example, it is likely that the gray wolf, red wolf, coyote, dingo, jackal, and domestic dog, which are six different species all belonging to the same biblical *kind,* all trace their lineage to the single pair of canines who left Noah's ark. You will rarely see these animals interbreed in the wild, but in captivity they have been known to interbreed and produce fertile offspring, thus revealing that they are indeed from the same original set of parents. So creationists do recognize microevolution (origin of new species within a kind), but not macroevolution (the changing of one kind into another through added information).

The changing of one kind into another would require an enormous amount of added genetic information in the genome. Yet no natural mechanism known to man can increase even the slightest amount of genetic information, let alone the amount of information necessary to produce the evolution from particles to people. Mutations simply do not add information to an organism's genome. "Neither chance, nor chance combined with natural selection, nor self-organizational processes have the causal power to produce information" (Strobel 237). Yet evolution teaches that random mutations plus natural selection generated information equivalent to 12,000,000 words accidently arranged in a meaningful order; and the word *accidently* is key here. That's why virtually all modern origin-of-life experts have utterly rejected the idea that life formed by random chance—evolution (Strobel 229). "Yet biblical creationists have no trouble explaining the presence of such complex information—it was created by the most intelligent Being in the universe" (Patterson 144).

An intelligent, First Cause, is necessary for life to exist. Darwin himself in his autobiography stated that he had issues getting past the First Cause. He wrote, "Another source of conviction is the existence of God, connected with the reason and not with the feelings, impresses me as having much more weight. This follows from the extreme difficulty or rather impossibility of conceiving this immense and wonderful universe, including man with his capacity of looking far backwards and far into futurity, as the result of blind chance or necessity. When thus reflecting I feel compelled to look to a First Cause having an intelligent mind in some degree analogous to that of man; and I deserve to be called a Theist" (*The Autobiography of Charles Darwin* 92-93).

Now, back to the cell, that which Darwin believed was the simplest unit on the planet. He even wrote in his *Origin of Species,* "If it could be demonstrated that any complex organ existed which could not possibly have been formed by numerous, successive, slight modifications, my theory would absolutely break down" (Strobel 197). In his book *Darwin's Black Box,* Michael Behe describes several examples of such systems that need all of their parts present from the beginning to function. Behe shows that a slow evolution of these living parts would have been impossible. What does this mean? It means that if Darwin knew what we know today about the complexity of the cell and its work in the human body, he would reject his own theory. Actually, one of the most extraordinary discoveries of the twentieth century was that DNA stores information in the form of a four-character digital code. Indeed, the cell has proven to be anything but the 'simplest unit' on the planet.

So let's take a quick look at the complexity of the cell. There are 75,000,000,000,000 cells in a human body. Each of these individual cells is more complicated than the most sophisticated, giant-sized computer ever invented because each tiny cell contains 200,000,000,000,000 tiny groups of atoms called molecules. The largest of these molecules is called DNA and carries hereditary information from parent to offspring. The length of each DNA strand in one cell is six feet long. If you stretched together the DNA strands in one human body it would cover the distance to the moon and back to earth over 400 times. Now, each of these 75,000,000,000,000 cells in each human body carries identical information, and the rate of error in cell division is equivalent to less than one letter wrong in a set of Britannica Encyclopedias. Also, "a one-square inch chip of DNA could store the information in over 7 billion Bibles—millions of times better than current technology" (Patterson 144). Does that sound to you like the simplest unit on the planet?

Given the above information, why do you suppose evolutionists still try to apply 10th century thinking (Darwinism) to 20th century reality? As Meyer stated, explanations from the era of the steamboat are no longer sufficient to explain the biological world of our information age? (Strobel 243).

Food for Thought: *Why do you suppose critics of the Bible, as they watched so many of their supposed biblical errors vanish through archeological discoveries, still refuse to admit the possibility that perhaps the remainder of their "supposed biblical errors" might also be wrong?*

Going Bananas!

According to one news report, researchers claim that humans and apes share 99.4% of the same DNA. Now this statistic is very misleading because it is based on a comparison of 97 genes from a human genome of 30,000. Other researchers have more accurately stated that the similarities between apes and human are approximately 95-96%. But even when you hear this 96% statistic, what do you automatically think? Isn't this figure intended to lead you to the conclusion that the ape is 96% human, or in reverse wording, the human 96% ape? With this in mind, consider the following: the evolutionist Steven Jones of England has pointed out that the banana (yes, that delicious piece of yellow fruit we all enjoy eating) shares 50% of their genes with humans. Using the same reasoning as apes being 96% human because of a 96% genome similarity, wouldn't that mean bananas are 50% human—or humans 50% bananas? Perhaps we should begin checking our bananas before we eat them, just to make sure they aren't developing eyes! Another like example is the similarities between a cloud and watermelon. Since a cloud is made up of almost 100% water, is it somehow related to a watermelon which is 98% water?

The real question we should be asking is, "Do the similarities between two objects prove that one of them evolved from the other?" Let's take a look at this concept. If you were walking down the street and a bicycle, motorcycle, automobile and pickup truck all passed by, would you automatically conclude that they evolved from each other because they all have wheels or other similar components? No, of course not. Your conclusion would be that they all had the same designer—man. Now let's apply this same principle to living creatures. Since the requirements are similar for living creatures, we would expect to find like structures based on a common Designer. Structures appear similar in living creatures (like eyes) because they were designed by the same entity (God) to accomplish the same purpose (to see). Another living example would be the kidneys of a skunk and the kidneys of a human. They look similar because they were designed by the same Designer to perform the same task (Patterson 71).

Now, thinking back to the ape being 96% human illustration, it's significant to note that it is not the similarities in genes that are important, but their differences. Remember that 4% difference between apes and humans? That meager little difference is equivalent to 40 large 500 page books worth of information (Sarfati vol. 2, pg. 186). That's no small amount of information!

Ask a few of your friends the following questions. When you mention the genetic similarities between the human and the banana, watch their facial reaction.

How closely related in genetic makeup would you guess the ape is to the human?

Would you be surprised if I told you that current studies show there is a 96% similarity between the human and ape genetic pool?

When an evolutionist gives you this 96% similar statistic, what conclusion do you think he wants you to reach?

Again, genetically speaking, how closely related in genetic makeup would you guess a banana is to a human?

Would you be surprised if I told you that a human's genetic makeup is 50% similar to that of a banana?

If you apply the same reasoning of "apes are 96% human" because of their "96% genetic similarities" to the banana/human relationship, what would your conclusion be?

Is this new knowledge of the banana being "50% similar in genetic makeup to humans" going to stop you from eating bananas? Why?

Consider the Odds

The more scientists learn about the complexity of the cell, the more they realize how ludicrous it is to believe it came about accidently by random chance. Consider the following from Patterson's book *Evolution Exposed*:

> "In 1860 a debate between Thomas Huxley and Bishop Samuel Wilberforce turned the tide in the public's acceptance of evolution. Bishop Wilberforce had published a review of Darwin's book of which Darwin commented, 'It is uncommonly clever; it picks out with skill all the most conjectural parts, and brings forward well all the difficulties.' Bishop Wilberforce presented several scientific arguments, and Huxley suggested that, given

enough time and material, six monkeys could type the 23rd Psalm simply by randomly punching the keys. It is reported that the bishop had no response, despite his training in mathematics. So what is the answer to Huxley's argument of time and chance?

If you give an ape a 50-key typewriter with letters, numbers, and punctuation, the chance of typing 'THE' is one in 50 x 50 x 50, or one in 125,000. At a rate of one strike per second this would take 34.72 hours. For the phrase 'THE LORD' the chance becomes 50 to the 8th power and requires 1,238,663.7 years. The entire Psalm requires 9.552 x 10 to the 1016th power of years to complete on average. The age of the universe is only 15 billion years according to evolutionists, so the probability is clearly outside of the realm of possibility.

When considering the probability of the assembly of a DNA molecule, the same problems arise. Harold J. Morowitz, professor of biophysics at Yale, has calculated that the formation of one *E. coli* bacteria in the universe at 10 to the power of 100 billion. Sir Fred Hoyle offered the analogy of a tornado passing through a junkyard and assembling a Boeing 747 or "nonsense of a high order" in his own words. Remember the law of biogenesis: life only comes from life. "Natural selection cannot be the mechanism that caused life to form from matter as it can only work on a complete living organism" (Patterson 146-147).

Hoyle also gave the analogy of life coming from nonlife as being equivalent to 50,000,000 blind men solving the Rubix Cube at the exact same moment (Holye 527). As the philosophical materialist Crick concluded, "An honest man, armed with all the knowledge available to us now, could only state that in some sense, the origin of life appears at the moment to be almost a miracle, so many are the conditions which would have had to have been satisfied to get things going" (Strobel 236).

It is interesting to note that the more impossible Darwin's theory becomes, the more time evolutionists tack on to the age of the earth. As the well-known evolutionary spokesperson George Wald stated, "Time is in fact the hero of the plot . . . . given so much time the 'impossible' becomes possible, the possible probable and the probable virtually certain. One has only to wait: time itself performs miracles" (Morris 41). Time, then, is presented as the hero of the plot. Yet in reality, time isn't the hero of the plot, but the villain. According to the most recent evolution time table the Big Bang occurred 10-20 billion years ago, our solar system formed 5 billion years ago, single-celled organisms came into existence *from nothing* around 3 to 4 billion years ago, multi-celled organisms developed approximately 1 billion years ago, human kind appeared on the scene around 1 to 3 million years ago, and modern civilization arrived about 5 to 10 thousand years ago (Morris 38). It's easy to see the problem here. Evolution would have to allow a hundred thousand trillion trillion trillion trillion trillion trillion trillion trillion trillion trillion years just for one short functional protein to randomly form. That's a ten with 125 zeros after it! It's far beyond the evolutionist's timeframe of 3 to 4 billion years for the single-celled organism. And that is only *ONE* protein molecule. A minimally complex cell would need between three hundred and five hundred protein molecules (Strobel 229).

Teachers: Complete worksheet Chapter 8: Creation versus Evolution—Puzzle 3

Chapter 9: Answering Darwin

Suggested Reading: Chapter 10 and 11 in *The Case for a Creator*

The Red Sea Crossing and Sodom and Gomorrah

The following are quotes by Charles Darwin taken directly from his autobiography, *The Autobiography of Charles Darwin.* Because these were problems Darwin had with Christianity and belief in a God who created, and even though they are not all immediately related to the creation of the world, I am going to use the next few chapters to speak on these precise issues so you will be more prepared to answer objections such as his.

> "But I had gradually come, by this time, to see that the Old Testament from its manifestly false history of the world, with the Tower of Babel, the rainbow as a sign, etc., etc., and from its attributing to God the feelings of a revengeful tyrant, was no more to be trusted than the sacred books of the Hinoos (Hindus), or the belief of any barbarian . . . By further reflecting that the clearest evidence would be requisite to make any sane man believe in the miracles by which Christianity is supported,--that the more we know of the fixed laws of nature the more incredible do miracles become . . . that the Gospels cannot be proved to have been written simultaneously with the events,--that they differ in many important details, far too important as it seemed to me to be admitted as the usual inaccuracies of eyewitnesses . . . I gradually came to disbelieve in Christianity as a divine revelation" (8586) and "much suffering in the world" (90).

Several topics are brought up in this one small passage of writing: the false history of the world, the Tower of Babel, the rainbow as a sign, God as a revengeful tyrant, the Bible as no more true than any other religious book of the world, the miracles of Christianity, the accuracy of the gospels, and much suffering in the world. Let's begin with his charge of the Bible being false history.

As we've seen in our study and reading of *The Case for a Creator,* scientific evidence is now siding against "in the beginning was a prebiotic soup," and with "In the beginning God created . . ." Although Darwin believed his theory of natural selection to have ample evidence to override the biblical story of creation, he was not privileged with the advanced scientific knowledge of the 21st century. As the scientific experts explained in *The Case for a Creator,* Darwin wasn't aware of how God can be seen in the sciences: cosmology, physics, biochemistry, biological evidences, consciousness, and etc. It is because of our current scientific knowledge in these areas that we now know the impossibility of life coming from non-life or of added genetic information being introduced into the cell without cause, of design equals Designer, of how everything that began to exist had to have a cause, of the laws and constants of physics, of the fine-tuning of the universe, and of how the laws of chemistry and physics cannot give explanation for our experience of consciousness. In today's scientific culture, it is Darwin's theory that is in serious question, not God's story of creation.

Let me combine Darwin's judgment of a "false history of the world" with his disbelief in miracles.

One of the greatest stories in the Old Testament is the Children of Israel's crossing of the Red Sea, which is certainly a miracle. It's one that people very often consider just a fanciful story to entertain ignorant religious adults and children. As a matter of fact, when my husband was attending Southwestern Baptist Theological Seminary and I Dallas Baptist University, the pastor's wife of our church shared their experience concerning this issue with us. They had attended a much more liberal seminary than SWBTS, and because they believed the Bible was the infallible and inerrant Word of God, they were a joke among their friends. Their acceptance of Bible stories such as the Red Sea crossing, the Divine destruction of Sodom and Gomorrah, and the literal fall of Jericho as actual history caused much amusement among their peers. When they were introduced by their friends to other seminary students, after their names was the short, sweet addition of, "This is the couple who believes God actually parted the Red Sea." This introduction would be followed with a slight laugh of amusement over their naiveté.

Check out the following website: www.arkdiscovery.com/red_sea_crossing.htm. On the left side of the page double click on the words *Red Sea Crossing*. You can either watch the video over the Red Sea crossing or read the information accompanying the website. Next, double click on the words *Sodom and Gomorrah* and again, either watch the video or read the material included. There are several other sites online where you can find even more pictures and information about these awesome, Bible validating discoveries. (Do an online search using the words: Bible Red Sea archeology.) After you have finished your research, complete the following Reading:

How does the trail to Nuweiba Beach and the beach itself both fit into the biblical story of the escape from Egypt, thus validating its authenticity? (Exodus 13 & 14)

Why does the traditional Reed Sea crossing site, the one supposedly dubbed the crossing site by Emperor Constantine and his mother due to a vision, not fit the biblical description?

Do you think God formed the underwater land bridge at the time of the crossing, or that perhaps He formed it when the earth was devastated with Noah's flood in preparation for Israel's future crossing?

Why do you think God only formed one site beneath the waters of the Red Sea that could have been used for people to walk across?

What are the archeological finds, both in the water and on the shore, that confirm Nuweiba Beach as being the authentic crossing site?

How does the current excavation site now known as *Sodom and Gomorrah* fit the biblical description found in Genesis 19?

What is extremely unique about the balls of sulfur that burned these cities?

Why is it easy for a true believer in God to accept the miracles of both the Old and New Testaments, yet so difficult for the unbeliever?

Food for Thought: *After seeing pictures of the discoveries of the chariot parts in the bottom of the Red Sea, and the discovery of cities whose destruction fits the biblical description of Sodom and Gomorrah, what are your thoughts?*

The Tower of Babel

In Genesis 10:8 we read that Nimrod became a *heroic warrior* before the Lord. The word translated *before* can also mean *against*, and this seems to fit more accurately with the passage. In other words, Nimrod campaigned with a spirit of defiance to rid the world of the shackles of true religion, or worship of the true and living God. Genesis 10:11 reads, "He went into Asshur (Assyria) and builded Nineveh," meaning he invaded Assyria and built up Nineveh. By every worldly standard, Nimrod could be considered a great political and military man in his day, yet the kingdom he built was a worldly system characterized by idolatry and opposition to the Lord.

The following passage in Genesis 11 does not teach that early mankind stupidly attempted to build a tower which would reach into outer space as many people suggest. The next time you're outside, stop and look up into the heavens. Do you believe anyone, especially someone with the intellect to become a great political and military leader, would honestly believe that he could build a tower so high it would actually reach into outer space? This teaching is a total misunderstanding of this passage.

Note verse four which reads, "Come, let us build ourselves a city, and a tower whose top *is* in the heavens; let us make a name for ourselves, lest we be scattered abroad over the face of the whole earth" (NKJV). Some versions include the words *may reach* in this verse instead of the italicized *is*. Whichever your version, these words are in italics to show they are supplied by the translators and are not in the original Hebrew text. A better rendering of this passage would be, "Come, let us build ourselves a city, and a tower *whose top is heaven*" or "a tower *topped with the heavens.*" In other words, astronomical and astrological data were to be associated with this tower, and its purpose was to worship the creation rather than the Creator (Wilmington 35). This appears to be man's first organized false religion, and the *against* in Genesis 10:8 reveals that Nimrod's purpose was to draw as many souls as possible away from the true and living God. *Wilmington's Guide to the Bible* states, "Archaeological evidence suggests that the Tower of Babel was in reality a building given over to astrology, or the heathen worship of the heavens" (Wilmington 35).

Let's continue with verse Genesis 11:5 which reads, "But the LORD came down to see the city and the tower which the sons of men had built" (NKJV). The words *came down* are actually sarcasm, indicating that man's most magnificent efforts were still puny in God's eyes. So why did God *come down?* He came down in judgment because man had become so flagrant in his defiance against Him that if immediate action wasn't taken, the truth of God's revelation might have been forever obliterated. Man's mistake was to believe that if he ruled God out of his thinking, he would rid himself of Him forever. He didn't realize that God will not permit any social order to last where He is omitted. So after taking the situation under consideration, God decided to judge the defiance of man by confusing his language, meaning He caused them to speak a variety of languages instead of just one (Genesis 11:7). The result of this judgment, people speaking a variety of languages, was indeed confusion, and the building of the tower of defiance toward God halted.

Now that we've taken a look at the circumstances surrounding the Tower of Babel, the question to ask is, "Is there any historical evidence that might support the authenticity of this story which Darwin openly denounced?" The answer again is yes, there is. Consider the following:

Wilmington's Guide to the Bible records the following: "Among the ruins of ancient Babylon is a building 153 feet high with a 400 foot base. It was constructed of dried bricks in seven stages, to correspond with the known planets to which they were dedicated. The lowermost was black, the color of Saturn, the next orange, for Jupiter, the third red, for Mars, and so on. These stages were surmounted by a lofty tower, on the summit of which were the signs of the Zodiac" (35). Upon the base of this building located just outside Baghdad the following words are inscribed, "A former king built, they reckon 42 ages past, but he did not complete its head. Since a remote time, people had abandoned it, without order expressing their words." Humm . . . Sound familiar?

Wilmington quotes Dr. Henry Morris as writing:

"As each family and tribal unit migrated away from Babel, not only did they each develop a distinctive culture, but also they each developed distinctive physical and biological characteristics. Since they would communicate only with members of their own family unit, there was no further possibility of marrying outside the family. Hence, it was necessary to establish new families composed of very close relatives, for several generations at least. It is well established genetically that variations take place very quickly in a small inbreeding population and very slowly in a large interbreeding population. In the latter, only the dominant genes will find common expression in the outward physical characteristics . . . even though the genetic factors for specifically distinctive characteristics are latent in the gene pool of the population. In a small population, however, the . . . genes will have opportunity to become openly expressed and even dominant under these circumstances. Thus, in a very few generations of such inbreeding, distinctive characteristics of skin color, height, hair texture, facial features, temperament, environmental adjustment, and others, could come to be associated with particular tribes and nations" (Wilmington 35).

In Genesis 10, you will find that the Bible gives the land locations where each of the descendants of Noah's sons—after the language divisions of the Tower of Babel—settled. The descendants of Ham, whose name means *dark* or *black,* are the Egyptians, Ethiopians, Libyans, Africans, and the other dark races, as well as the Canaanites who once lived in the land now occupied by Israel. The descendants of Japheth, whose name means *bright* or *fair,* are the Greeks and the people who lived in the islands of the sea and who settled Europe and Russia. The descendants of Shem, whose name means *dusky* or *olive colored,* are the Semitic people—the Jews, Arabs, and Persians. Isn't it interesting that the skin coloring of the descendants of these three men match the meaning of their specific name? This suggests that perhaps Noah named his sons according to a unique physical appearance they were all born with—the color of their skin.

From the 16 grandsons of Noah people migrated throughout Asia and the Far East (Genesis 10). They traveled south to Australia and northeast to the shores of America. Everywhere they traveled they carried the original knowledge of the ancient world, including the story of the most recent catastrophic event—the flood of Noah's day. Seeing the historical connection to the lands and people who settled our world helps to validate our scriptures as authentic history.

The third evidence that supports the Tower of Babel is the various languages themselves. Emeritus Professor Cavalli-Sforza, described as the world's leading expert on human population genetics for the past 55 years has been studying the way our human race has spread, how the various races developed, and about our cultures and various languages. Cavalli-Sforza believes that language is the major characteristic distinguishing us from apes. He writes, "Children are born with the propensity and ability to learn a language . . . it requires a precise anatomical and neurological foundation," which apes don't have, and which Cavalli-Sforza believes was present in our earliest ancestors (Sforza 174).

> If languages had evolved in a stepping stone manner as the Darwinian Theory suggests, we would expect some to be more primitive than others. Yet Cavalli-Sforza states that there are no primitive languages. Every human language is very complex, with the grammar and syntax of some primitive peoples being even richer and more precise than languages like English or Spanish (Cavalli-Sforza Ref. 6, pg. 59).

> Also, all known languages can be grouped into 17 language families (amazingly close to Noah's 16 grandsons in number), or 17 original languages, but linguists have trouble reconstructing the relationship of these languages above their family level, and some have ruled it out altogether. Cavalli-Sforza believes that most language families appear to have developed during a brief period between 6,000 to 25,000 years ago, yet he also stated that all of these languages were present in our earliest ancestors. This doesn't fit into Darwin's theory which teaches that our nearest common ancestors lived about 5,000,000 years ago (Cavalli-Sforza Ref. 6, pg. 145).

> In summary, the current support that we have indicating that the Tower of Babel was actually history and not just a fanciful story is (1) archeological remains of what could well have been the actual tower, (2) the division and separation of mankind just as the Bible states, and (3) the existence of 17 different languages that seem to have no evolutionary stage with one descending from another, all of which abruptly came into existence between 6,000 to 25,000 years ago.

If you're interested in a more precise division of where Noah's son's settled, skim through the following: (copied)

Genesis 10:1-3 (The sons of Japheth were Gomer, Magog, Madai, Javan, Tubal, Meshech, Tiras.)

Gomer: Noah's first grandson was Gomer. Josephus, an ancient historian, indicates that the Gauls were first called Gomerites. France was known as Gaul. Gomerites also migrated to Great Britain. The Welsh language (Wales) was once called Gomeraeg. Descendants of Gomer eventually came to America from Spain, France and Great Britain. Gomer's sons were Ashkenaz (Germany),

Riphaht and Togarmah (Turkey). Turkey is the modern name for Togarmah. Ashkenaz is the Hebrew word for Germany.

Magog was the second grandson mentioned. The Greeks were called Magogites Scythians. This was the ancient name for the countries of Romania and Ukraine.

Madai was the next grandson mentioned. His descendants were the Medes, people who settled in modern-day Iran. During the time of Daniel, they were known as the Medes and Persians. These people also settled in the land of India.

Javan is the next grandson. The Hebrew word "Javan" means Greece. (Genesis 10:4) Javan's sons were Elisians. The Apostle Paul was from the city of Tarsus in Asia Minor, or southern Turkey today. Kittim is the Bible name for Cyprus. Dodena was the seat of worship for Jupiter, a Greek god. Jupiter is a name derived from Japheth.

Tuban is the next grandson. His descendants in the land of Georgia (former USSR) were called Tabali, or Thobelites. The capital of Georgia is named Tbilisi. Farther north, across the Caucasus Mountains, were the river Tobol and the famous city Tobolsk.

Meshech is the next grandson. His name is the ancient name for Moscow. An area near Moscow is still named the Meschera Lowland.

Tiras was the next grandson. His descendants were named Thirasians, later named Thracians by the Greeks. The Greek god of war was named Thor among these people. Their land included the New Testament lands of Thrace and Thyatira, basically the land north of Greece, between the Adriatic and Black Seas.

Genesis 10:6-21 (The sons of Ham were Cush, Mizraim, Phut and Canaan.)

Southwest Asia and Africa marks the home of Cush. The name Cush is translated Ethiopia in the Bible. Even today many people in this area call themselves Cushites. Cush begot Nimrod, the founder of Babel which was later named Babylon, and today is called Baghdad, Iraq. It was here at the Tower of Babel, a ziggurat of the ancient world, that God confused the languages. After this confusion, people groups, defined by their language, began to migrate to the far corners of the world.

Mizraim is the Hebrew word for Egypt. In Genesis 50:11, Egypt is called Abel Mizraim. He was the ancestor of Philistim who fathered the Philistines, the same ones who lived in the land of Palestine. Mizraim also fathered Heth, the founder of the Hittite empire, and Jebus the father of the Jebusites. Their name gave rise to the name of the city of Jerusalem.

Phut is the Hebrew word for Libya.

Canaan is the land of Israel and Jordan today. It includes the land promised to Abraham and his descendants in Genesis 12.

Genesis 10:2-31 (The sons of Shem were Elam, Assur, Arphaxad, Lud and Aram.)

Elam is the ancient name for Persia (remember the Medes and Persians) and referred to Iran. During Jesus' day these people were called the Elamites.

Assur is the Hebrew word for Assyria. The descendants were the dreaded Assyrians. An angel killed 85,000 of them during the days of King Hezekiah. They were also the inhabitants of Nineveh to whom Jonah was sent.

Chaldea was the ancient name for the area in eastern Iraq, just north of Saudi Arabia. The founder of Chaldea was Ariphurra, a second spelling for Arphaxad. His son was Eber who gave his name to the Hebrew people through the line of Abraham, who originally came from Ur of the Chaldees.

Lud was the brother who traveled west. His name gave rise to the area of Lydia in western Turkey. Its capital was the city of Sardis, to whom John wrote a warning in the book of Revelation.

The land along the coast north of Israel is known as Syria, the Hebrew word for Aram. Aram's descendants spoke Aramaic, a language known throughout the world and spoken by Christ when he was on the cross.

God, a Revengeful Tyrant?

Darwin's accusation of God being a revengeful tyrant shows his total lack of scriptural understanding concerning the attributes of the Creator. When the rich young ruler came to Jesus, he said, "Good Teacher, What good thing shall I do that I might have eternal life. Jesus' response was, "Why do you call me Good? No one is good but One, that is, God" (Matthew 19:16—NKJV)." A careful study of this passage lets us know that Jesus wasn't saying He wasn't good, or that He wasn't God, but instead was attempting to lead this young man to the correct knowledge of who He really was—the good and perfect God.

Yes, God is good. He is perfect. And as so many so often state, He is love. These are all attributes that most people freely attribute to Him. But what Darwin, as well as many others seem to want to ignore, is that He is also a holy and just God, and He would not be a holy and just God if He allowed wickedness to go unpunished. You see, it is the very fact that He is a holy and just God that demands His punishment of evil. God, being Creator, had the right to establish whatever penalty He wanted for sin, and the penalty He established is death—both physical and spiritual. "But isn't that a harsh penalty?" you ask. No, actually it's the perfect penalty. You see, it was the very establishment of death as the penalty for sin that made it possible for the Perfect Son of God to pay that penalty for us.

Yes, God's love for us was so great that He didn't want us to suffer the just punishment we deserve, both physical and spiritual death. That's why Jesus came to this earth in human form. It wasn't so He could play the revengeful tyrant and zap anyone who annoyed Him, it was so He could pay the horrible debt for our sins with His death on Calvary. When Mel Gibson's *The Passion of the Christ* came out, many people criticized him for going overboard with the blood; yet for those who have studied Jesus' crucifixion more in depth, it is apparent that Gibson's portrayal doesn't measure up to the real suffering Christ endured.

In Isaiah 52:14 we read, "So His visage (appearance) was marred more than any man, And his form more than the sons of men" (NKJV). This was Isaiah's prophecy concerning the physical abuse the Messiah would suffer both leading up to and during his stent on Calvary. After the physical beatings (Jews had the limit of 39 lashes, but Romans didn't, and it was a Roman crucifixion), after the hematidrosis he suffered in the garden (Luke 22:44), after his beard being yanked out by the handfuls (Isaiah 50:6), after the crown of thorns being placed on his head (Matthew 27:29), after the trauma of spikes being driven into his wrists and feet (Psalm 22:16), and after the plural effusion (Luke 19:24), He was such a bloody mass of meat that He didn't even look human (Isaiah 52:14). If you had personally known the man called Jesus who hung on that cross, you would not have recognized Him as your friend. Do you know what's so amazing about all of this? At any time He could have halted this physical abuse by calling ten legions of angels (Matthew 26:53), yet He chose to endure that suffering for us. I've heard it often said that it wasn't the nails that kept Christ on Calvary; it was His love for you and me. How true that statement is! Now, does a God who would suffer this greatly for His creation sound like a revengeful tyrant to you?

Why does God Allow Suffering?

The very existence of suffering has caused many, Darwin included, to reject the idea of a Good and Perfect God who created. Why? Because they can't understand why a God whose attributes are those of the God of the Bible would allow the innocent to suffer and evil to triumph. Their argument: if God is really good, all-powerful and all-knowing as the Bible teaches, why doesn't He stop the wickedness and violence that is so rampant in this evil world? Why does He allow the innocent to suffer?

To answer these questions we must first travel back in time to the paradise God created for man, the garden called Eden. This was the world—a world without sin, suffering or evil—where God desired man to call home. Living in this garden was a sweet time for man and his wife. It was a time when life was easy, food was plenteous, where man was kept busy caring for God's creation, and best of all, where there was intimate communion with God their Creator. While in this garden God had placed only one restriction upon man, to not eat of the Tree of the Knowledge of Good and Evil. The purpose for allowing man access to this tree, yet forbidding him to eat from it, wasn't to set a trap, but because God wanted man to obey Him by choice. He wanted man to have free will, to love and worship him on his own accord. God knew that without a way to break a rule there would have been no free will, no choice to be made.

Until the day that man took of the forbidden fruit (and we are not told what type of fruit that was), there was no pain, death, or suffering in this world. But once God's one rule had been broken, this penalty for sin was fully activated. Death, being that penalty, came into existence; and this wasn't just a physical death, but a spiritual death as well. Note that God said, "In the day that you eat of this tree you shall surely die" (Genesis 2:16). God's declaration was that man would die that very day, yet Adam lived for another 930 years after eating from this tree. Was God wrong in His declaration of immediate death? No, He wasn't. Adam and Eve did die that very day, but the death they suffered immediately wasn't physical, but spiritual. That was the dreadful moment when man's spiritual unity with the holy and just God was severed.

The results of this spiritual death were many: communication between man and his Creator was forever changed, man would no longer search for his significance through his Creator but would now look to his own performance and the opinions of others for his self-esteem, and of utmost importance, man would now be separated from the Creator God for all eternity. We've already discussed how, because of His love for us, God provided the penalty for our sin so we wouldn't be separated from Him, so now let's go back to Darwin's original argument: why would God allow suffering? Think about it for a moment. Had God not placed physical death, which includes suffering, as the consequence for our sins, mankind would have lived forever, perfectly content in his wicked condition. It was actually because of His love for us that God ran man out of the paradise before He could eat from the Tree of Life, so we wouldn't live forever suffering in these sinful, physical bodies.

Before you judge this next statement, I want you to fully weigh what I am saying. "It was because of his love for us that He allowed death and suffering to enter our world." Explanation: if God had allowed Adam and Eve's lives to be without pain and suffering, do you think they—being now spiritually separated from God and bound for an eternity in hell—would have sought after God. If life had been perfect on this earth, why would they have tried to restore their relationship with their Creator?

Now, you tell me which is more important, to have a paradise without pain and suffering on this earth for a few measly years, or to recognize our plight due to wickedness and suffering and thus search for God while He may still be found so that we can be reunited with Him for all eternity. Let me repeat this, God allows death and suffering in this world for the precise purpose of compelling us to get our hearts right with Him before it's too late and we suffer the just punishment for our sins. A few years of pain and suffering to drive me to my knees so I'll spend an eternity in God's presence; that sounds like a wonderful trade to me.

Christianity and the God of the Bible

Although Darwin was raised in the Christian faith, he was never truly a Christian. His, as Paul states in 2 Corinthians 3:6, was head knowledge and not heart knowledge. And once again, as Paul predicted would be the outcome of children raised with head knowledge (letter of the law) and no heart knowledge (never accepted Christ as their Lord and Savior), he abandoned the faith as he grew older. Because Darwin had no personal relationship with the Creator of the universe, he eventually came to believe that He didn't exist. The natural progression of unbelief in God is the rejection of His Word, the Holy Scriptures. After all, if there is no God, then the Bible is nothing more than a concoction of man's imagination. That's why Darwin was able to equate the Bible as being on the same level as any other religious holy book, and Christianity itself on the same playing field with the religions of this world. So how do we answer Darwin's argument? What makes the Bible and Christianity not only superior to other religions or religious books, but the actual true religion and authentic book of God?

There are several different accusations included in Darwin's argument, so I will deal with each of them individually. First of all, Darwin equated Christianity as merely one of the religions of the world. I must begin here because Christianity isn't just a religion. The *religions of the world* all have one point in common, they are man trying to work his way to God through various means. True Christianity, on the other hand, is not man trying to work his way to God, but God coming down to save man. Christianity is not just following a code of conduct or a set of rules; it is having a personal relationship with the God of creation. But for argument sake we're going to place Christianity into the same category with the other religions of the world.

My sophomore year of college was at Southwest Baptist University in Bolivar, Missouri. One day, half way through my first semester, a group of us students got into a heavy conversation. Our debate ended up with two sides, those who believed the Bible to be the inerrant, God-breathed, inspired Word of God, and those who believed it contained errors. *(By errors I don't mean misspelling and typos that have crept in through the millenniums, but doctrinal and historical inaccuracies. The ancient manuscripts called the Dead Sea Scrolls match our current Bible translations nearly perfectly, with only slight variations, none of which experts agree change any basic Christian truth.)* Finally, when those on the opposing side weren't able to convince us that the Bible did indeed contain historical and doctrinal errors, one girl stared straight into my eyes and made the statement, "You do realize that parts of the Bible were taken from the Koran?" At that time I was hardly aware of what the Koran was, much less how to argue her point. All I could do was stubbornly revert back to my original argument, that the Bible was indeed the inerrant, inspired Word of God. Her statement, stated as *proven fact*, bothered me for years. How could parts of my Bible, God's Holy Word, have been stolen from the Muslim Koran—a false religion with a false holy book? It wasn't until years later that I discovered the truth to this lie.

Consider the following: There is ample proof that our Old Testament, the Hebrew books of history and prophecy, was completed in its current format around the time 400 B.C. when the Great Synagogue met after the Babylonian captivity. This group of men included the priest Ezra, the builder of the walls surrounding Jerusalem and eventual governor Nehemiah, Haggai, Zechariah, and Malachi. At the Council of Jamnia in 90 A.D. the Old Testament scriptures were canonized or closed, meaning no more writings would be accepted into what had become known as the 36 books of the Old Testament—Genesis through Malachi.

The final book to be written of the New Testament was John's *Revelation* of end times, and since the Apostle John died in 100 A.D., *Revelation* was obviously written prior to this date. Because of many heresies and false prophets that were arising in the early church days, in 397 A.D. our church fathers met together to close the canon of the New Testament writings before these heresies could infiltrate God's Word. This means that our entire Scripture, the 36 books of the Old Testament and 27 books of the New Testament were completed in their current format prior to the year 100 A.D., with all 66 books being canonized by the year 397 A.D. These facts aren't just made up, but are easily verified as actual history.

Now consider this, Mohammad, the author of the Koran, wasn't born until the year 570 A.D., and he didn't begin writing the Koran until 610 A.D. So, given this evidence, you tell me how my Bible stole from the Koran! The Bible was completed in its finished format over 500 years before the writing of the Koran even began. No, the Bible didn't steal from the Koran. The exact opposite is true; the Koran stole from the Bible, and we have the historical and archeological evidence to prove it.

Additional confirmation of the Bible:

First, the Bible was written over a period of 1600 years by over 40 different authors, yet its central theme can be summarized with only three words: *God's Redemptive Plan.* How would it have been possible for this many men, over such a vast number of years, living in a variety of different areas to write a collection of writings that, in their final analysis, all agree with each other and point toward one theme? When compared with the other ancient religious writings, these 66 books were so far superior that they literally "rose above" the rest. They had the mark of Divine inspiration. In other words, it wasn't man who inspired and brought together the writings of the Old and New Testaments, it was God. He was the originator and engineer of what has become known as His Word, the Christian Bible.

Second, if the Bible isn't the inspired Word of God, how is it that 500 of its recorded 1000 prophecies have already come true, and the 500 yet to be fulfilled all deal with the second coming of Christ? The book of Daniel alone records historical prophecies that were so accurate that many critics claimed it couldn't have been written during the time in which Daniel lived (6th century B.C.). They used its hundreds of fulfilled prophecies as their evidence, because no human could be that accurate predicting the future. When the *Dead Sea Scrolls* were discovered in the Qumran caves, they proved that the book of Daniel was indeed written during the 6th century B.C. exactly as it claimed, because it was written in eastern Aramaic, which is different from western Aramaic and was only used during that specific century. Another excellent example that must be included in the "historical accuracy of fulfilled prophecy category" is the book of Isaiah. It contains a large number of prophesies concerning the birth, ministry, and death of the Messiah. And again, with the discovery of the *Dead Sea Scrolls,* we now have the entire manuscript of Isaiah, prophecies included, dating back to 125 B.C. That's 120 years before the birth of Christ!

How does the nonbeliever explain this new historical evidence concerning the Messianic prophecies of Isaiah? Some have suggested, "Perhaps He fulfilled them by chance." But that is a literal impossibility. Why? Because the calculated odds of only eight of these prophecies being fulfilled by accident are one chance in one hundred million billion, which is millions of times greater than the total number of people who have ever lived (Strobel 246).

Third, what outside corroborating evidence do we have that validates the Bible and ancient Christian literature concerning the life of Christ? Another way to consider this is, if every copy of the New Testament and all of the other ancient Christian writings were burned, what would we know about Jesus from secular histories such as the writings of Josephus, the Talmud, Tacitus, Pliny the Younger, and others? Without these Christian writings we would know that Jesus was a Jewish teacher who lived around the turn of the millennium, that many people believed He performed healings and exorcisms, and multitudes believed He was the Messiah. We would also know that He was rejected by the Jewish leaders, crucified under Pontius Pilate during the reign of Tiberius Caesar, yet despite His shameful death of crucifixion his followers believed He was still alive. We would know that His followers spread beyond Palestine so that multitudes of them even lived in Rome by A.D.64, that all kinds of people from all stations of life worshiped Him as God (Strobel 115), and that His followers believed with such surety that He had risen from the dead that they were willing to go to horrific martyrdom themselves rather than denounce Him as their risen Lord. Finally, we would know that multitudes of Jews were willing to give up their religious tradition—a tradition that had held their nation together for centuries while in exile— to become followers of Christ, and that these individuals were also willing to be considered traitors and denounced by their own families for accepting Jesus as their Messiah.

Fourth, before the printing press was invented, preservation of written material was a much more difficult task and the materials would deteriorate quickly, yet when the ancient manuscripts (handwritten copies) of the Bible are compared with those of other works of antiquity, the Bible stands unrivaled. No other document in history even comes close! More than 5000 Greek New Testament documents have been catalogued, while the number two book in manuscript authority, the *Illiad of Homer,* has only 643 manuscripts (Strobel 78). "We have copies commencing within a couple of generations from the writing of the originals, whereas in the case of other ancient texts, maybe five, eight, or ten centuries elapsed between the original and the earliest surviving copy"(Strobel 76). "Even if we lost all the Greek manuscripts and the early translations, we could still reproduce the contents of the New Testament from the multiplicity of quotations in commentaries, sermons, letters, and so forth of the early church fathers" (Strobel 76)

Fifth, through the years various people have attempted to disprove the Bible's authenticity, its reliability, and its recorded accuracy, yet their efforts have been unsuccessful. As we discussed in an earlier topic, the development of archeology has helped to disprove much of the criticism about the Bible's accuracy. The discovery of over 17,000 tablets with more than 5,000 geographic names listed in them verified both places and people previously not found mentioned outside Scripture, silencing many of the Bible's critics.

When examining the historical reliability and accuracy of any ancient piece of literature, there are three tests which can be applied: (1) ***the bibliographical test***—(how close the copies are to the original writing; the more manuscripts you have, the easier it is to recreate the original and check out any errors or discrepancies); (2) ***the internal evidence test***—(a document is innocent until proven guilty, meaning it is considered accurate until an error is proven; the nearer the witnesses are to the event, both chronological and geographical, the more accurate it is considered; the ultimate test of the apostles' accuracy was their willingness to die horrible deaths for their belief in what they witnessed and wrote); and (3) **the eternal evidence test**—(are there sources other than the document which confirm the inner testimony contained in the document? This would include literary sources, archeological sources, as well as other historians from that era confirming the writing's accuracy.) When the Bible is tested using these three categories, it passes with flying colors!

In *The Verdict of History,* historian Gary Habermas details a total of thirty-nine ancient sources documenting the life of Jesus, from where he gathered more than 100 reported facts concerning Jesus' life, teachings, crucifixion and resurrection. Twenty-four of these sources cited by Habermas, including seven secular sources and several of the earliest creeds of the church, specifically concern the divine nature of Jesus (Strobel 120).

Now, let's continue to Darwin's charge that the gospels differ in the details concerning the life of Jesus. To begin this rebuttal, I want you to picture a court of law. In any trial, if the witnesses all say the exact same thing, even use wording that is too similar, what does the jury and judge automatically suspect? They suspect a conspiracy. It gives the appearance that the witnesses got together before the trial and decided what they were going to tell the jury. In Lee Strobel's book, *The Case for Christ,* he quotes Craig Blomberg, who is widely considered to be one of the country's foremost authorities on the gospels, as saying, "Ironically, if the gospels had been identical to each other, word for word, this would have raised charges that the authors had conspired among themselves to coordinate their stories in advance, and that would have cast doubt on them. . . . If the gospels were too consistent, that in itself would invalidate them as independent witnesses. People would they say we really only have one testimony that everybody else is just parroting" (Strobel 58).

Also, the only way to judge any writing is according to the standard of the time in which it was written. One study suggested that writings in the ancient Middle East allowed a variance in story telling of 10% to 40%, as long as the teller didn't omit any key details or add details which were inaccurate. If the story teller didn't follow these guidelines, any person from the crowd could speak up and correct the story. This percentage, 10 to 40 percent, is right in the category of the variances of the gospel stories (Strobel 54-55).

Now, back to that court of law. It's not until the jury pieces together all of the individual eyewitness accounts that they are able to figure out the true events. The same rule applies to the four gospels. They were all four written by different men with different perspectives, and it's not until you collect all of the details and put them together that you get the full picture of what actually happened.

I would like you to do a quick experiment. Make three columns on a sheet of paper and then look up the following references. Write every detail recorded in that specific reference concerning the miracle of Jesus walking on water in one of the columns. Don't add any details to any one of the columns that is not mentioned in that specific gospel. After you have finished listing the complete set of details recorded in all three gospels, as a jury in a court of law would do, summarize the finished product or complete story of Jesus walking on water. In this summary be sure to include every detail from each of the three gospels. Your three references are Matthew 14:22-36, Mark 6:45-56, and John 6:15-25.

Miracles

Darwin's final argument against there being a God was his unbelief in miracles. What exactly is a miracle? I've often heard people attribute the term miracle very loosely to events that do not qualify. It is not a miracle that "someone looked your way," or that "it didn't rain on game day." A miracle is an event that defies a law of nature. Many of you can cite times in your lives when something happened that defied a law of nature, such as a tumor vanishing. One day while a high school Bible class I was teaching was studying the Red Sea crossing, a young lady spoke up and questioned, "Why don't miracles like that happen today?" Of course my answer was, "They do." Obviously, no great body of water has divided in recent days, but there have been miracles on a frequent basis. Did you realize that West Point won't even permit their students to study Israel's 6 Day War because the events that led to their victory are so impossible there's no way to explain them? They just ignore that it ever happened.

Most miracles that occur today are not as huge as those recorded in the scriptures, but they do happen often on an individual level. I could personally share with you about a time when my brother's nose was obviously broken, bleeding profusely and smashed on his face, and when mom placed her hand on it and prayed the bleeding stopped suddenly and he was fine; or of the time when my dad saw through a one-inch thick solid wooden gate to see that my life was in danger and was able to rescue me just before I was trampled by some angry steer; or of the time when a wicked man who wanted to hurt my sister was throwing his entire body against the door of an old decrepit trailer in an attempt to gain entrance—a door that would normally open with the slightest pressure even when locked—yet the door held firm until the authorities arrived. Then there was the time when my sisters were driving in a horrible thunderstorm and found themselves within feet of a head-on collision with a semi when suddenly it vanished, only later to discover they had driven through a tornado that had "lifted a semi from the road and set it down a mile away"; and the time when a car security system's horn sounded just in time to warn me of danger, only later to discover that that specific car had no security horn system. All of these are events that either defied a law of nature, or perhaps used a law of nature but were clearly directed by the hand of God. These were all actual events that happened in my life or in the lives of my family, and I'm certain many of you could share like experiences.

But for someone who doesn't want to believe in God, no amount of miraculous events will cause them to become a believer. That's why in the parable of the rich man and Lazarus, Abraham told the rich man that, "Even though One come back from the dead, they will not believe" (Luke 16:31). If a man has determined in his heart to reject God, no amount of the miraculous will cause him to change his mind. It's very significant that Abraham used that illustration, "though One come back from the dead," because that is exactly what happened a short time later, and still those with hardened hearts didn't believe. That very event, the resurrection of our Lord Jesus Christ, is one of the greatest miracles ever. It's the miracle that skeptics, knowing that if they disprove the resurrection of Christ all of Christianity tumbles, have often set out to attack with fervor. Yet it's interesting to note that many atheists in history who have specifically targeted the resurrection of Christ have themselves, after a thorough and honest search of the events, become believers. As stated by Michael Green in *The Case for Christ,* "The appearances of Jesus are as well authenticated as anything in antiquity . . . There can be no rational doubt that they occurred, and that the main reason why Christians became sure of the resurrection in the earliest days was just this, They could say with assurance, 'We have seen the Lord.' They knew it was he" (Strobel 325).

An example of some of the evidence surrounding His resurrection is as follows: I have often seen pictures of the empty tomb with one or two overweight, out of shape Roman guards slumped over sleeping next to the entrance. But in reality, nothing could have been farther from the truth. A Roman guard was anywhere from 12 to 16 men, and these men were of the most elite trained soldiers in the army. They were the "cream of Rome's crop," so to say. The standards by which these guards worked were extremely high. If a guard fell asleep on duty, the death penalty applied. If a prisoner escaped, again the death penalty applied. In light of this, the first act the guard would have done upon arriving at the tomb would have been to make sure their prisoner, even though He was merely a dead body, was in the tomb. Next, when the Bible says the soldiers "sealed the tomb" it means that they performed an actual act of sealing the tomb. This was accomplished by placing hot wax on both the stone in front of the tomb and on the tomb itself. Next, they would stretch a piece of string or a hair and press it into that hot wax in both places. As long as the hair or string was in place, unbroken, they had evidence that the body was still there. Also, in that day if a guard was caught sleeping it was the responsibility of a fellow soldier to run him through with his sword, even as he slept.

When Jesus' body disappeared, the Jewish religious leaders spread the word that "while the guard slept his disciples came and stole it." Consider this for a moment. We're supposed to believe that 12 to 16 of the most highly qualified soldiers in the Roman army all fell asleep at the exact same moment; otherwise they would have been one by one exterminating each other. Also, have you ever heard a rock screeching against rock? Once again, while the guard slept, the disciples supposedly snuck into camp and rolled the stone away, and during this process the sound of a 2000 pound boulder screeching against the cave, which would have been noise enough to have awakened the dead (excuse the pun), didn't alert the guard as to what was happening.

Let's evaluate just these two points for a moment. The above facts surrounding Jesus' resurrection are found in the Bible, but are they located anywhere else? Is there any secular evidence that there was a guard placed at the tomb and a missing body? The answer to that question is yes. Even today if you ask an orthodox Jew what happened to Jesus' body they will tell you that while the guard slept His disciples came and stole it away. This is recorded in ancient

Jewish literature as well. That, in and of itself, is proof that there was a _guard_ positioned at the tomb, and that there was a _missing body_.

These are only two of a multitude of facts surrounding Jesus' death, burial, and resurrection that have persuaded unbelievers who honestly checked into the evidence, both biblically and historically, to become believers. The evidence for the resurrection is so great that, as Moreland pointed out in *The Case for Christ*, "in a short period of time not just one Jew but an entire community of at least ten thousand Jews were willing to give up the . . . five key practices that had served them sociologically and theologically for so many centuries? . . . they had seen Jesus risen from the dead" (Strobel 340). If you would like to know more, Lee Strobel has written a book titled, *The Case for Christ* that is loaded with evidence just like this. I would highly recommend reading his book!

To find out more about the miracle of the Six Day War do an online search of the **Six Day War miracle** and a site called *The Six Day War: Recognizing the Miracle – Judaism – Israel National News* will appear. It's fascinating!

Food for Thought: *Has God performed a true physical miracle in your life that you would like to share with me? Please email your miracle experience to me at www.rocklanpublications.com.*

Teachers: Complete worksheet Chapter 9: Quiz over Reading Material

Chapter 10: Consequences of Darwin's Theory

Suggested Reading: *Darwin's Deadly Legacy* by Tom DeRosa

Beliefs Matter

Beliefs matter. They matter because they influence the way we relate to people around us and to God. If a person believes they are nothing more than the "byproduct of chance events brought about by random mutations in a pool of primordial slime," they will pattern their life accordingly. Their decisions and actions will stem directly from that belief. A perfect example was the young lady I mentioned previously who worked at my sister's veterinarian clinic. Her world view was so warped by her wrong beliefs that she was unable to decide which was more important, a human life or the life of a dog. Remember the Columbine killers? They believed that murdering someone was nothing more than "scattering molecules" and "survival of the fittest." They took Darwin's teachings to heart. To their thirteen victims who were slaughtered that day, and to their victim's families and friends, these two young men's beliefs mattered.

If you read Darwin's autobiography, it is easy to see that he would never have supported men like the Columbine killers; nor would he have given his stamp of approval to godless tyrants like Hitler who rule with terror and blood. He was an everyday loving husband and father. So where did he go wrong? How did this everyday man end up devising a theory that would influence two young men to go on a shooting rampage and godless world leaders to slaughter millions? The answer to that question can be traced to Darwin's lack of faith in the Creator. He had no room for God in his life. Yes, in his earlier years he attended a church, but he wasn't a true believer, and the church he attended wasn't a real Christian church.

How do I know this? Because Darwin attended the Unitarian Church of England, a church whose beliefs had long rejected the authority of God's Word and basic Christian doctrine. This was a church that rejected the deity of Christ—which is an absolute requirement for true biblical faith. Instead, its belief focused on each individual's ability to improve themselves without reliance on God or His Word. This belief alone, the absence of God's Word as the ultimate authority, opened the door for Darwin's warped conclusions concerning the world around him. Two additional key biblical doctrines that the Unitarian Church had long abandoned were the Trinity and the fall of man; by rejecting the Trinity they abandon the possibility of salvation, and by rejecting the idea that man was naturally wicked and in need of a Savior they eliminated the need for an ultimate place of punishment for those who rejected God's salvation—hell. After rejecting the deity of Christ along with these key biblical doctrines, in essence rejecting the authority of God's Word, one wonders why they even bothered to call themselves *Christian*.

This was the false religion Darwin grew up in, and with a lack of genuine faith in his Creator he had no foundation upon which to stand when his daughter, ten-year-old Annie, succumbed to the terrible disease of tuberculosis (supposed diagnosis by physicians of today). Having no true relationship with God, and in bitterness of heart, he replaced the Creator of his false religion with a new religion, *natural selection*, thus devising a theory that would become a magnet for those who wished to abandon all belief in God. Although Darwin's abandonment of the Creator doesn't appear to have been with the desire of "now I can do what I want without consequence," many who have latched on to his theory have done so for that precise reason. After all, natural selection did away with the need for God, and without a God to answer to for your actions, you can do anything you desire; without a God to dictate the standards of right and wrong, you can create your own.

That is what is so dangerous about the theory of man being a byproduct of random chance. It does away with God! Thus it gives a justified foundation for men like the Columbine killers, Hitler, and others to create their own standard of right and wrong, and if their newly devised standard happens to include the murder of 13, or the murder of millions, who are we—a mere product of random chance—to say their standard is wrong? Here's the dilemma, without an Ultimate Authority (God) who sets the standards, what makes one standard superior or more acceptable than another?

Darwin and Hitler weren't contemporaries, so how is Darwin's theory of natural selection related to Hitler's murderous genocide? Evolution classifies men in the same manner that it classifies animals, which is what Hitler used to justify the mass extermination of *inferior races*. It's important to note that this extreme prejudice wasn't merely an innocent byproduct of Darwin's theory that others pinned to his name; it originated with Darwin himself when he drew his tree of life and theorized that good would come from death by way of natural selection, it was promoted by Darwin when he classified black Africans, Australian Aborigines, and Tasmanians on the lower limbs of his evolutionary tree, and it was practiced by Darwin when he referred to those with dark skin as "degraded," saying he would rather have descended from a monkey than such a "savage". Darwin even predicted that one day the "civilized" races would rise up and exterminate the "savage" races (DeRosa 127). Sound familiar?

When Hitler rose to power in 1933 he had one agenda, the enactment of his radical Nazi racial philosophy built on Darwinian evolution. As a result of Hitler's belief in evolution, he set in motion the machinery to assist nature in speeding up the evolutionary process. His agenda: to eliminate the weak, impure blood, disabled, sick, Jews and Gypsies. What nature supposedly took millennia to accomplish through natural selection, he was attempting to accomplish in mere decades. Five months after rising to power, on January 1, 1934, he ordered the sterilization of 400,000 Germans who were deemed *unfit*. Included in this number were the feeble-minded and those suffering with schizophrenia, manic depression, Huntington's chorea, epilepsy, hereditary body deformities, deafness, hereditary blindness and alcoholism. In 1935 he passed the Nuremberg Laws which prohibited marriage between the *inferior race* of the Jews with the *superior race* of the Germans, and he stripped the Jews of their German citizenship (DeRosa 124). One of his key goals was to kill the 11,000,000 Jews living in Europe, thus preventing the spread of their *inferior blood* into the *pure German population*.

So was Darwin, this everyday loving husband and father, aware of this danger his proposed theory could propagate? Yes, he was. Numerous of his contemporaries warned him of the lasting effects of such a godless theory, yet he refused to listen, and to date his refusal to listen has cost close to 100 million people their lives through leaders who used his theory to justify mass genocide (DeRosa 10).

Evolutionists might argue that his refusal to listen was only because he was following the evidence, but this isn't true. Natural selection wasn't the only direction the scientific evidence pointed. Richard Owens, the leading British anatomist who initially helped Darwin identify some of the specimens he'd collected on the Galapagos Islands, was one of the men who warned Darwin of the lasting consequences of such a godless proposal. Having assisted in identifying these specimens, Owens had seen the same Galapagos evidence as Darwin, yet he attributed the common structures within a species as evidence of a common Creator, not a common ancestor. He also believed that each species had its own "organizing energy" that would dictate just how far mutations within that species could travel. As a result, along with many of Darwin's contemporaries, Owens flatly rejected the idea of one kind evolving into another. When *Origin of the Species* went public in 1859, he became one of its strongest outspoken critics (DeRosa 31).

Going back to my original question, how could this everyday loving husband and father devise such a godless theory that would wreak murderous havoc in our world for centuries to come? It was because of his blatant denial of the existence of a Supreme Being, which then caused a dilemma. If *in the beginning God didn't create,* then where did life come from? Darwin knew that, in such a magnificent and awe-inspiring world as ours, the only way to justify his atheism was to devise another means by which life came into existence—a means that left God out. The late Stephen Jay Gould, an outspoken atheistic who continually refused to debate creationist scientists even for much monetary gain (Morris 8), showed how Darwin's intended purpose was to destroy the idea of a divine deity. Natural selection was the answer to both of Darwin's dilemmas; it allowed the abandonment of God and gave an alternative means by which man was created. Once developed, his new theory not only helped to settle his own atheistic mindset, it also gave a multitude of others who wished to denounce a divine Creator the intellectual means by which to justify their unbelief. As Richard Dawkins stated, ". . . before Darwin it was impossible to be an intellectually fulfilled atheistic" (Strobel 19).

Is it not amazing that Darwin, a man who devised a scientifically unsupported theory which led to the deaths of multitudes, is praised worldwide for his advanced scientific thinking, while Richard Owens, his contemporary who was far ahead of his counterpart according to today's scientific cellular (DNA) knowledge, is basically unknown?

Darwin and Eugenics

Darwin's cousin, Francis Galton, is the founder of what is known as eugenics. What is eugenics? It's the "movement devoted to improving the human species through the control of hereditary factors in mating" (Webster). After reading *Origin of Species,* Galton wrote that his cousin's theory "first put me . . . in harmony with nature." Then, being "in harmony with nature," he proceeded to develop the idea of "favored stock" among the human race. He wrote, "The possibility of improving the race of a nation depends on the power of increasing the productivity of the best stock," and by suggesting the idea of limiting marriages to the union of well-born partners and prohibiting the marriages of the "unfit," he claimed we could accomplish quickly and kindly what nature does slowly and ruthlessly (DeRosa 141). By proposing this idea he was lowering the breeding of humans to the same level as cattle, yet Darwin praised his work. It should not be surprising that it was his essay *Eugenics as a Factor in Religion* that Hitler later used for support in the slaughtering of millions.

It is important to note that Darwin's theory of evolution and Dalton's development of eugenics are themselves cousins—two sides of the same coin. Darwin may not have agreed with everything his cousin believed in regard to his evolutionary theory, but eugenics was his own theory's logical conclusion. So how did Darwin and Dalton decide which races were inferior and which were superior? They used superficial characteristics such as skin color, eye color, facial features, and the shape of the nose. Cavalli-Sforza, the expert in human genetic variation mentioned earlier in this course, noted that these characteristics are only skin deep. He wrote, "It is because they are external that these racial differences strike us so forcibly, and we automatically assume that difference of similar magnitude exist below the surface in the rest of our genetic makeup. This is simply not so; the remainder of our genetic makeup hardly differs at all" (DeRosa 126). Sforza actually stated that there is more genetic variability between people of the same race than between people of different races.

Darwin, not being an actual physician and having little experience in human paleontology, barrowed greatly from Ernest Haeckel's *Natural History of Creation* in classifying the order of human descent. Haeckel, a very controversial German physician and devout evolutionist, faked his embryo research data and falsified drawings of various vertebrate embryos in an effort to persuade people toward the theory of natural selection. Continuing his propaganda, and without any scientific evidence to base his conclusion on, he drew six human and six simian facial profiles, arranging them by the supposed order of their evolutionary ranking of those most human to those least human. His drawings placed Europeans as the most highly evolved, East Asians second, with the continuing order of Fuegians, Australian Aborigines, black Africans, Tasmanians, and finally gorillas, and other apes (DeRosa 118).

"Haeckel had exaggerated the data, doctored images, censored information, used only what supported his conclusion, and created deceptive drawings that were complete misrepresentations" (DeRosa 147). Even though his works were proven to be fraudulent the same year they were produced, 1868, Darwin praised him saying, "almost all the conclusions at which I arrived I find confirmed by this naturalist, whose knowledge on many points is much fuller than mine" (DeRosa 147). If Darwin were honestly weighing the evidence, why would he have associated himself with such a controversial individual? Why would he have used data proven fraudulent almost as soon as it was published to support his own theory?

Research both Charles Davenport and Margaret Sanger using the internet. When you finish, consider how both of these individuals put Dalton's eugenics into practice in our country.

Darwin's Trail of Tears

Among those who have suffered much because of Darwin's theory of classifying people into superior and inferior categories are the Aborigines and the natives of Tasmania. They, being the groups categorized lowest on his scale of human evolution, were once hunted and slaughtered for various reasons. Land owners in Australia who believed Darwin's theory justified their murderous actions with the reasoning that, "If it's OK to kill wild dogs as pests, then it's OK to kill sub-humans." If you've seen the movie *Quigley Down Under,* you've seen a good picture of what was actually happening on the continent of Australia.

In 1924, the New York Times ran an article about the natives of Tasmania titled, *Kindred of Stone Age Men Discovered on Australian Island—Missing Links with Mankind in Early Dawn of History."* The natives of Tasmania, along with the Australian Aborigines, were now seen as valuable research specimen because they were "the missing links" and "proof of evolution." As a result some were captured alive to be studied or used in exhibits, thousands (possibly up to 10,000) of their graves were desecrated when their bodies were exhumed from their burial grounds, others were killed right on the spot, and many were driven into swamps and then shot. Their hunters had been given precise instructions on how to appropriately skin them and prepare their skulls to be specimens for museums around the world. Even until recently, if an Aborigine married a non-Aborigine in Australia the child from their union was considered more advanced than the Aborigine parent and therefore forcibly taken away and placed in a foster home (Manne). This practice didn't stop until the late 1960's, and then there wasn't an official apology from the Australian government until 2008 (Ham).

Research the stories of Ota Benga, a pygmy from the Congo, and Princess Truganini, a Tasmanian Aborigine.

Chapter 11: In Conclusion

Two Great Men

Two babies, both destined to be great by worldly standards, were born that day. It was February 12, 1809. One was born into poverty, the other into wealth; one into a family of lowly status, the other into society's elite; one into true faith in the Creator, the other into pretense of faith. These two babies would grow into men separated by far more than the vast distance between their continents; they would be separated by the enormity of their differing world views. One would become such a man of faith that his knees would callus from bending in prayer to his Maker; the other would devise a theory to sway millions away from the Creator. The man with callused knees would lead a nation with the concept of equality to all men and would push hard for that belief; the other, although himself against slavery, would popularize a world view that would enslave multitudes and cause the deaths of millions. While one wrote a proclamation declaring equality for all men, the other wrote a book titled *On the Origin of Species,* with the subtitle of *The Preservation of Favoured Races in the Struggle for Life.* As one was fighting a war to free men of "dark skin" from slavery; the other called those with dark skin "degraded," and declared he would rather have descended from a monkey than such a "savage." The first man would give his life to reunite a divided nation; the other would cause division not only in his own country but in all countries for centuries to come.

Two hundred years have now passed since the renowned day of their births, and while the first man, President Abraham Lincoln, is celebrated as the leader who led a nation to abolish slavery because "all men are created equal"; the second man, Charles Darwin, is celebrated as the man who abolished the need for a Creator. Ideas are not without consequences. Abraham Lincoln's ideas led to free men from slavery; while Darwin's assumption that men evolved by random chance led Josef Stalin, a mass murderer of multitudes, to become an atheist as a young man while reading his works in seminary; it inspired Karl Marx, who offered to dedicate his book *Das Kapital* to Darwin, to state that Darwin's theory "contains the basis in natural history for our view . . ."; and it influenced Hitler, a devout evolutionist who instructed his troops in evolution by providing them books by Darwin and Friedrich Nietzsche, to the idea of inferior races and thus the slaughter of millions in an effort to speed the evolutionary process. These Darwinian enthusiasts, some of the world's most notorious and depraved leaders, along with Mao, Pol Pot, and other communist leaders, have murdered close to 100 million people, and all compliments of a theory which lessened the value of human life to an accident of random chance, thus no greater than that of any animal[1].

These two men, President Abraham Lincoln and Charles Darwin, great by worldly standards, left two vastly differing legacies. How is it that the first, Abraham Lincoln, is briefly mentioned in many public classroom settings, while the other, Charles Darwin, a racist man who promoted racist ideas that led to and justified horrific, mass genocide, is frequently praised for "opening the minds of many" (Schweikart; Allen)?

Final Analysis

As you have seen throughout the process of taking this course, there is much evidence that points toward "In the beginning God created," and none that points *exclusively* toward "in the beginning was a primordial slime." In *The Case for a Creator,* Jonathan Wells quoted Henry Gee, the chief science writer for *Nature* as saying, ". . . all the fossil evidence for human evolution between ten and five million years ago—several thousand generations of living creatures—can be fitted into a small box" (Strobel 63). Think about this for a moment. We have countless dinosaur skeletal remains, which according to the evolutionist timetable died out 65 to 70 million years ago; yet we have basically no pre-human skeletal remains, which they claim lived only five to ten million years ago. And that "small box" of evidence Gee was referring to, it can be interpreted in a manner which supports the biblical story of creation just as easily as it can be used to support evolution. It depends upon the interpreting scientist's individual bias as to which theory he chooses.

When confronted with this lack of evidence by creationists, evolutionists often resort to name calling and ridicule. Even the late Stephen Jay Gould, a prominent American paleontologist, evolutionary biologist, and historian, referred angrily to "the scourge of creationism," yet he refused to debate a qualified creation scientist because it would be, as he put it, "a mistake to dignify creationism and its scientists in this way." It seems to me that an avid evolutionist who supposedly had all the evidence he needed to prove his theory would gladly have confronted his opponents in an open debate. Yet instead of accepting a debate to prove his ideology, he criticized those with differing views, calling them "fundamentalists who call themselves 'creation scientists,' with their usual mixture of cynicism and ignorance." Gould, while refusing to accept creationist debates and pronouncing evolution as fact, in his 1,433 page book title, *The Mismeasure of Man*, failed to give one piece of actual evidence of macroevolution—the type of evolution that is the very foundation of Darwin's theory (Morris: Evolutionary Arrogance 9).

This name-calling and ridicule is not rare among evolutionists. When someone who is determined to push their belief regardless of the evidence can't answer their critics, name-calling and ridicule is often their key tool. Another example of such behavior is that of Ernest Mayrs who, although he, too, failed to cite even one example of macroevolution in his own textbook, dared to pronounce that "every knowing person agrees that man is descended from the apes" (Morris: Evolutionary Arrogance 9). This is evolutionists' key problem; they declare their theory as fact without absolute proof and then resort to ugly behavior towards those who don't accept their declaration. You tell me, why would any "knowing person" accept a theory which has not been proven true with undeniable facts and which counters known laws of science?

While writing this final lesson, an article published in USA Today was given to me. In this article, two professors at a supposedly religious university were belittling organizations such as Answers in Genesis, while at the same time presenting their case that you can believe in evolution without it damaging your faith in God. They proceeded to make comments like, "Almost everyone in the scientific community, including its many religious believers, now accepts that life has evolved over the past 4 billion years," and "evidence for evolution has become overwhelming," and finally "the fossil record has provided evidence of compelling transitional species." As you have seen in this course, these statements are outright lies. When Lee Strobel questioned Dr. Stephen C.

Meyer about the idea of life forming by random chance, Dr. Meyer replied, "Virtually all origin-of-life *experts* have utterly rejected that approach." He continued to expound his statement by saying, "Yes, it's true that this scenario is still alive among people who don't know all the facts, but there's no merit to it" (Strobel 227).

For these two professors, or any other members of the educated or media world, to make misleading and spiritually harmful statements to sway impressionable youth of our age away from God's truth is not only total propaganda, it is nothing short of sheer wickedness. Almost everyone in the scientific community does not believe life evolved from non-life, there is no overwhelming evidence that evolution is true, and the fossil record has not proven the existence of transitional species—in fact, it has proven the exact opposite.

Probably the most important lesson I want you to learn from this course is to not simply take someone else's word as fact just because they have a Ph.D. after their name or a charismatic personality. What we, as believers in Christ, must always remember is that any time a teaching or idea of this world counters God's Word, it is not God's Word that is in error. As Christians, our ultimate authority is the Word of God. God, and God alone, was there on the six days of creation. He, and only He, knows how and when He created the heavens and the earth; and He chose to give us the details of that great event in his word, the *Bible*. Why would such an awesome and magnificent Creator bother to give us His Word? It is because of His great love for us. He wants us to know the truth so we can be set free from this world's wickedness, from its way of thinking and living and eventually spend an eternity with Him in His Heaven. Thank God for His Word, the *Bible*, that pilots us through this temporary life of wickedness and into an eternity with Him.

In closing, remember what William Lane Craig said concerning the actual scientific evidence of the 21st century, ". . . I think it's indisputable that there has never been a time in history when the hard evidence of science was more confirmatory of belief in God than today" (Strobel 123).

Everyone has a choice to make! You can either accept God's Word and His gift of salvation through His Son the Lord Jesus Christ, or you can reject His Word and believe the world's lies—and don't kid yourself, not to choose is to choose. By not making a choice for Christ you are choosing the world. Stop and think about your own heart for just a moment. Have you made a decision for Christ? Are you sure that when you die you will spend eternity in His presence? Confess your sins to Him. Open your heart to the One who created you, who loves you so much He gave His life on Calvary so your sins could be forgiven and you could be reunited with Him in eternity.

If you haven't made this decision, or if you're not sure about your relationship with Christ, a simple prayer in faith is all it takes to become one of his children. The following is a short example: *"Dear Lord Jesus, I know that I'm a sinner. I believe that You died on the cross to pay the price for my sins so I could live with You in eternity. I now confess my sins to You. Forgive me of those sins, come into my heart, be my Lord and my Savior. Right now, I give all of myself to You. I want to live my life for You. Thank you, Jesus, for saving me."*

Teachers: Complete worksheet Chapter 11: Final Exam

Worksheet for Biblical CEU's

Chapter 2: What Does the Bible Actually Teach?

Summarize each of the following verses and their significance in your own words. When you are finished, compare your summary with the information provided below. How thorough were you in your evaluation?

John 1:1-3 and Colossians 1:15-18—

Genesis 1:1—

Psalms 33:6-9—

Mark 10:3-6—

Genesis 2:7—

Genesis 1:31—

Romans 5:12 and 1 Corinthians 15:21-22—

2 Peter 3:3-6—

Romans 8:22—

Acts 3:20-21—

Corinthians 15:45-49—

Chapter 3: Why Should Christians Study Evolution?

1. Why is it important for Christians to know the Bible?

2. Give two reasons why it is important for Christians to understand the theory of evolution.

3. Define and explain the two types of science.

4. Why is it important to understand that evolution fits into the historical realm of science?

5. What type of evolution does the Bible support? Give an example with your answer.

6. What is the difference between laws and theories?

7. Give two ways the law of biogenesis defies evolution?

8. Cause and effect implies that a design must have what? Give an example with your answer.

9. Give an example of the probability of evolution being true.

10. What type of evolution is required for Darwin's theory of evolution to be true?

Chapter 4: Creation Versus Evolution—Puzzle 1

1. Popularized a theory that paved the way for God to be removed in the minds of many: _ _ _ _ _.

2. Science that depends on assumptions concerning the past: _ _ _ _ _ _ _ _ _ _ _ -- _ _ _ _ _ _ _.

3. Abbreviation for the true "witch hunters" of the Scopes Trial: _ _ _ _.

4. Someone's guess that has not been proven true: _ _ _ _ _ _.

5. When used with the words *evening* and *morning*, a number or ordinal, it always means a solar day: _ _ _.

6. The third son of Adam and Eve's mentioned in scriptures—but not their 3rd child: _ _ _ _.

7. Cave men with slight bone issues who were once thought to be the missing link: _ _ _ _ _ _ _ _ _ _ _ _.

8. A deliberate hoax pawned off as proof of evolution for 50 years: _ _ _ _ _ _ _ _ -- _ _ _.

9. In the Old Testament scriptures this word always means a set of solar days: _ _ _ _ _.

10. Science that is testable and repeatable and potentially falsifiable: _ _ _ _ _ _ _ _ _ _ _ -- _ _ _ _ _ _.

11. A fictitious character in the movie *Inherit the Wind* who was used to make Christians look ignorant: _ _ _ _ _ _ _ _ _ -- _ _ _ _ _.

12. Believed that if they killed their classmates, they would merely be "scattering molecules": _ _ _ _ _ _ _ _ _ -- _ _ _ _ _ _ _.

13. According to Jewish tradition, Adam and Eve had this many children: _ _ _ _ _ _ -- _ _ _ _.

14. Intakes carbon dioxide and lets out oxygen, which allows earth to support human life: _ _ _ _ _ _. 15. He and his entire family were reconstructed from a single tooth—that of an extinct pig: _ _ _ _ _ _ _ _ -- _ _ _.

16. God created this on the fourth day of creation: _ _ _ _ _ -- _ _ _ _ _ _ _.

17. Assumed by scientists to be the first woman who ever lived from whom all women descended: _ _ _ _ _ _ _ _ _ _ _ _ _ --- _ _ _.

18. Life never comes from nonlife: _ _ _ -- _ _ -- _ _ _ _ _ _ _ _ _ _.

19. Proven by science to be true: _ _ _.

20. A grossly apelike figure hailed as the missing link because tools were found nearby: _ _ _ _.

21. False drawings of embryos designed to prove the evolution from one species to another which are today still in text books even though they were proven inaccurate nearly 150 years ago: _ _ _ _ _ _ ' _ -- _ _ _ _ _ _ _ _.

22. A tree Darwin designed to picture the order of descent from one species to another that has literally been turned up-side down by the discovery known as the Cambrian Explosion: _ _ _ _ _ _' _-- _ _ _ _-- _ _-- _ _ _ _.

23. An experiment that some evolutionists claim produced organic molecules, thus the possibility of life; yet when performed using the accurate atmospheric chemicals actually produced Cyanide, thus eliminating any possibility of producing life: _ _ _ _ _ _-- _ _ _ _ _ _ _ _ _ _.

24. Evolutionists wrongfully claim this creature to be proof of evolution because they say it is "half-bird and half-reptile": _ _ _ _ _ _ _ _ _ _ _ _ _.

25. Instead of proceeding from observation to conclusion, the conclusion interprets the observation and is then used to "prove" the conclusion: _ _ _ _ _ _ _ _-- _ _ _ _ _ _ _ _ _.

Chapter 5: Creation versus Evolution—Puzzle 2

1. Our universe must have had a beginning, and therefore, a _ _ u _ _.

2. The everyday functioning and coincidences of our universe is without question a _ _r _ _ _ _.

3. Scientific evidence actually supports _h _ _ _ _ _ _ belief.

4. The main issue with accurately predicting _ _ _t events is, "We weren't there."

5. A name of God which is plural in form but singular in nature and is the first biblical reference to the Trinity is _ _ _ _ _m.

6. God transcends the universe and is therefore above the _ _ _s of nature.

7. Romans 1:20 tells us that God's eternal power and divine nature can be seen and understood through - - - -r -.

8. In the atheistic viewpoint our universe popped into existence out of _o _ _ _ _ _ with absolutely no explanation at all.

9. _ _-- _i _ _ _ _ is a word the Bible uses that means God spoke the universe into existence out of nothing.

10. The basic structure of the universe is balanced on a _ _ _ _ _' _--e _ _ _ for life to exist.

11. Albert Einstein developed his general theory of _ _l _ _ _ _ _ _ _ _ in 1915, which is a theory that doesn't allow for a static universe.

12. Science and faith are not at _ _r as so many people like to suggest.

13. The cause of the universe must transcend matter, space, and _ _ _ _ _.

14. The theory whose p _ _ _ _ _ _ _ _ _ _ most accurately fit the evidence is the most likely true.

15. "There are more than _ _ _ _ _ _ separate physical or cosmological parameters that require precise calibrations in order to produce a life-sustaining universe" (Strobel 132).

16. Allan Rex Sandage has been dubbed the "Grand Old Man of _ _ _ _ _ _o _ _."

17. The fine-tuning of our universe cannot be explained as a cosmic -c _ _ _ _ _ _ _.

18. Many scientists of this modern era have been driven to _ _i _ _ by their very work.

19. The Bible teaches that the decay and deterioration we see in our world is the result of _ _ _s.

20. To begin with a specific theory, interpret your data according to that theory, and then claim that your conclusion verifies your theory is called c _ _ _ _ _ _ _-- _ _ _ _ _ _ _ _ _ _.

21. Information in the cell requires an intelligent _ _ _ _ _ _ _ _.

22. The assumption since ancient Greek time was that the world was _t _ _ _ _ _ _.

23. Creation and evolution are two different _ _r _ _ views.

24. The C _ _ _ _ _ _ _ _--E _ _ _ _ _ _ _ _ _ provides not only a negative case against macroevolution, but a positive argument for the biblical story of creation.

25. The _ _ _ _ _ argument states that whatever begins to exist has a cause, the universe began to exist, therefore the universe had a cause.

Chapter 6: Mid-way Opportunity

1. The main issue with accurately predicting past events is, "_____ weren't there."

2. Scientific evidence actually supports a _____ belief.

3. The Cause of the universe must transcend matter, space, and _____.

4. The everyday functioning and coincidences of our universe is without question a _____.

5. God transcends the universe and is therefore above the _____ of nature.

6. Atheists believe that our universe popped into existence out of _____ and without a cause.

7. Information in the cell requires an intelligent _____.

8. Many scientists of this modern era have been driven to _____ by their very work.

9. The _____ argument states that whatever began to exist has a cause, the universe began to exist, and therefore the universe has a Cause.

10. The _____ Explosion provides a negative case for evolution and a positive case for creation.

11. What are five inescapable conclusions we must admit if Darwinism is true?

   There is no _____.
   There is no _____ after death.
   There is no absolute foundation for _____ or wrong.
   There is no ultimate _____ for life.
   People don't really have a free _____.

Short Answer:

1. Who were the true witch hunters of the Scopes Trial?

2. When *yom* is used in the Old Testament with the words evening or morning, or with a number or ordinal, it always refers to a what?

3. In the Old Testament scriptures when the word *yamin* is used it is always a reference to a set of solar days. What is the significance of this when compared to Exodus 20:8?

4. The Neanderthal man is generally accepted to be nothing more than what?

5. What missing link was the product of a complete fraud; yet was passed off as proof of evolution for more than 50 years?

6. What is the difference between operational and historical science?

7. What missing link was created from the tooth of an extinct pig?

8. Peter prophesied that in the end time scoffers would arise who would willfully forget what two historical events?

9. What biblical problems does it cause when you make the assumption that Seth was the third son born to Adam and Eve?

10. What two ways does the law of biogenesis defy evolution?

11. What would be the characteristics of a Cause with the intelligence to create a universe like ours?

12. What does *ex nihilo* mean?

13. Explain how evolutionists use circular reasoning to "prove" their theory is true?

14. What is wrong with dating an organic object such as a rock and calling your conclusion the *absolute age?*

15. Explain why planet earth can be called the *privileged planet*. (Stroble 132).

16. Give three scientific principles that were taught in the scriptures long before man was aware of their truthfulness? (Check back in topic *Science Taught in God's Word.*)

17. What are five serious theological issues with trying to mesh evolution into the biblical story of creation? (Check back in topic *Serious Theological Issues.*)

Short Essay:

1. Write a paragraph explaining how Hollywood's bias can be seen in the movie *Inherit the Wind*.

2. How would you use the information we've discussed so far to witness to an evolutionist friend?

Chapter 7: The *Limiting Age Factor*

Example: Too little sediment of all kinds in earth's crust: The time needed to accumulate the entire sedimentary crust on the earth's surface is only _____, far too few for the theory of evolution (Morris 88).

1. Galaxies wind themselves up too fast: If our galaxy was more than a _____ old it would be a featureless disc of stars instead of its present spiral shape (Humphreys 1).

2. Earth's rotation slowing down: The earth is presently spinning at a speed of 1046.6 miles per hour at the equator, but every ten months the scientific community sets the atomic clock back one second because it is slowing down. If the earth is slowing down, that means it used to be going faster. Even _____, which is far less than is required for the theory of evolution to be true, the earth would have been spinning too fast to sustain life (Hamilton 1).

3. Moon is moving away from the earth at 2 to 3 inches per year: Since the moon affects our ocean tides, the closer it is to us the greater the force of gravity. Only a _____ the moon would have been close enough to cause the tides to drown the entire surface of the earth twice a day. (You can only drown once!)

4. Not enough salt in the sea: The current level of salt in the oceans would have accumulated in _____, far less than is required for evolution to be true (Humphreys 2).

5. Continents would have been flattened by erosion: With the current rate of the erosion of the continents, all land would be reduced to sea level in merely _____. If the uplift and erosion on our earth had been continuing for even two or three times that 14,000,000 in the past, all of our sedimentary rock would be gone by now (Morris 88).

6. Not enough mud on the sea floor: Twenty billion tons of dirt and rock are deposited in the oceans each year. This material accumulates as loose sediment on the hard lava-formed rock of the ocean floor. With the average depth of all ocean sediment being less than 400 meters, and allowing for the sediment that is removed by the sliding of the ocean floor beneath the continents (only a few cm/year), all the sediment currently on the ocean floor would have accumulated in less than _____, far less than is necessary for the theory of evolution to be true (Humphreys 2).

7. Comets disintegrate too quickly: "According to evolutionary theory, comets are supposed to be the same age as the solar system, about five billion years. Yet each time a comet orbits close to the sun, it loses so much of its material that it could not survive much longer than about 100,000 years. Many comets have typical ages of _____" (Humphreys 2), which fits perfectly into the biblical story of creation.

8. Earth's magnetic field decays too fast: Life would have been impossible had the earth's magnetic field decayed along its present trend for even _____ (Morris 80).

9. Biological material decays too fast: "DNA experts insist that DNA cannot exist in natural environments longer than _____, yet intact strands of DNA appear to have been recovered from fossils allegedly much older: Neanderthal bones, insects in amber, and even from dinosaur fossils. Bacteria allegedly 250,000,000 years old apparently have been revived

with no DNA damage. Soft tissue and blood cells from a dinosaur have astonished experts" (Humphreys 3).

10. Underground oil deposits are under too much pressure: Geologists believe that there is 20,000 pounds of oil pressure per square inch beneath our planet's surface. At a pressure this great, our planet's crust should have cracked around _____ after it formed.

11. Jupiter, Saturn, Uranus, Neptune, and Pluto are cooling off: If these planets are 4.5 billion years old as evolution teaches, they should have cooled off long ago. Their current temperature fits perfectly into the _____ of the creation story (Brown, Walt. 1995).

12. Too few supernova remnants: Supernovas, or violently-exploding stars, cause remnants of gas and dust to expand outward rapidly. In the nearby parts of our galaxy, where we can observe the remnants from the explosions, we find evidence for only about 200 supernovas. This number is consistent with only about _____ of supernovas (Humphreys 1).

13. Too much helium in minerals: Newly-measured rates of helium loss from zircon crystals show that it has been leaking for approximately _____ (Humphreys 3).

14. Too little moon dust: With no rain, wind, or water, the dust that falls on the moon's surface stays right there, that's why much time was spent concocting landing pedestals on the first spacecraft to minimize the distance it would sink into the dust. Yet when it landed, there was only about an inch of dust. This measurement fits perfectly into the creationist timeframe of a _____, but it is far less than the 150 feet that was expected for the theory of evolution to be true (Morris 88).

15. Written history is too short: "According to evolutionists, Stone Age *Homo sapiens* existed for 190,000 years before beginning to make written records about 4,000 to 5,000 years ago. Prehistoric man built magnificent monuments, made beautiful cave paintings, and kept records of lunar phases, why would he wait nearly _____ before using these same skills to record history" (Humphreys 5)?

16. Too much carbon 14 in deep geologic strata: No carbon 14 atoms should exist in any carbon older than 250,000 years, yet it is impossible to find any natural source of carbon below Ice Age strata that does not contain significant amounts of carbon 14. Recent discoveries give further evidence that the earth is _____ of years old (Humphreys 4).

17. Not enough Stone Age skeletons: Using the evolutionist's scenario, prehistoric man should have buried at least 8,000,000,000 of their dead. Also, if their evolutionary time scale is correct, buried bones should be able to last for much longer than 200,000 years, so many of the supposed 8,000,000,000 skeletons should be just beneath the surface, along with their buried artifacts. Yet only a few thousand have been found. This signifies that the _____ (Humphreys 4).

18. Many strata are too tightly bent: Strata in many mountainous areas that are thousands of feet deep are bent and folded into hairpin shapes. "The conventional geologic time scale says these formations were deeply buried and solidified for *hundreds of millions of years* before they were bent. Yet the folding occurred without cracking, with radii so small that the entire

formation had to be still wet and unsolidified when the bending occurred. This implies that the folding occurred _____ after deposition" (Humphreys 3).

19. Fossil radioactivity shortens geologic "ages" to a few years: Radiohalos are fossil evidence of radioactive decay. _____ in the Colorado plateau _____ apart as required by the conventional geological time scale (Humphreys 3).

Chapter 8: Creation versus Evolution—Puzzle 3

1. New findings in astronomy suggest that our planet is indeed _ _ _ c _ _ _.

2. Everything about the earth, its location, size, composition, structure, and surroundings testify to the "degree to which our planet is exquisitely and precariously" _ _l _ _ _ _ _ _.

3. To survive humans need _ _ _ _ _ _ _ -- _ _ _ elements and a bacterium of about sixteen.

4. Most galaxies fall into the _ _ _ _ p _ _ _ _ _ category.

5. The probability of life inhabiting other planets keeps declining as we learn more about our _ _ _ _ _ _ s _.

6. What really matters is that earth is _o _ _ _ _ _ in the exact place to allow life to exist.

7. Scientists have discovered that Jupiter actually acts as a s _ _ _ _ _ to protect us from too many comet impacts.

8. Our moon contributes in unexpected ways to provide a stable _n _ _ _ _ _ _ _ _ _ for our planet.

9. The evidence of design is evident from the far reaches of the M _ _ _ _ -- W _ _ down to the inner core of our planet.

10. In *The Case for a Creator,* Gonzaliz concluded, ". . . the universe was designed for observers living in places where they can make scientific _i _ _ _ _ _ _ _ _ _."

11. A _ _ _ _ _ -- B _ _ is a term scientists use to describe a system or machine they find interesting but can't explain.

12. Darwin stated that if "any complex organ existed which could not possibly have been formed by numerous, successive, slight _ _ _ _ f _ _ _ _ _ _ _ _, my theory would absolutely break down."

13. Life is based on molecular m _ _ _ _ _ _ _.

14. The only force known to be able to make irreducibly complex machines is I _ _ _ _ _ _ _ _ _ _ design.

15. Science should be the search for _r _ _ _ and not merely the search for materialistic explanations to explain how life came about.

16. One of the many proofs that the Bible is God's authentic word is the many _ _ _ _ _ t _ _ _ _ statements that were written in it long before our world was aware of their truthfulness.

17. We can limit the age of the earth through observable scientific data by using what's known as the L _ _ _ _ _ _ _ _ -A _ _ --F _ _ _ _ _.

18. A c _ _ _ _ _ _ _ _ _ _ _ mechanism for the formation of the Grand Canyon seems most likely. (catastrophic)

19. In order for the traditional theory for the Grand Canyon's formation to be accurate, the Colorado River would have had to have run _ _h _ _ _.

20. If you take all 50 different types of dinosaurs known to man when they were at young adult stage, their average size would have been that of a _ _e _ _.

21. An _ _ _ -- _g _ would have been the natural result of a global flood.

22. _ _ _ _ _ _s _ _ _ _ _ is the hero dinosaur of Hollywood and many books, yet he never even existed.

23. Fossil evidence indicates that T-Rex walked in a stooped-over position, probably waddled like a duck, and would have needed dentures had he attacked other large dinosaurs because the roots of his _ _ _ _ _ were only one inch deep.

24. _ _ _ _ _ _ _ _ _ _ is the dinosaur recorded in the book of Job about which God said, ". . . nothing on earth is his equal."

25. _ _ _ _ _ _ _ _ is a dinosaur recorded in the book of Job whose name means "kingly, gigantic beast."

Chapter 9: Quiz over Reading Material

1. According to Darwinists, when the brain reached a certain level of structure and complexity, people became _____, meaning they suddenly developed subjectivity, feelings, hopes, point- of-view, and self-awareness.

2. In 1871, Thomas Huxley believed that the mind was a function of _____ when it attained a certain degree of organization.

3. A computer will never attain consciousness because all it can do is "shuffle _____."

4. The existence of _____ in human beings is strong evidence against Darwinism and for a Creator.

5. After performing surgery on more than 1000 epileptic patients, Wilder Penfield encountered concrete evidence that the brain and mind are actually distinct from each other although clearly connected. What was that evidence? _____

6. What is dualism? _____

7. MIT's Marvin Minsky stated that the brain was merely a "computer made of _____."

8. What did the year-long British study given in the text provide evidence of? _____

9. What was that evidence? _____

10. Consciousness consists of what six entities? _____

11. What did Jesus describe the soul and body as being? _____

12. What are three logical implications if _____ is true?

13. "The scientist can know about the brain by studying it, but he can't know about the _____ without asking the person to reveal it."

14. Computers have _____ intelligence, not true intelligence.

15. Consciousness is what causes behavior in conscious beings, but _____ circuitry is what causes behavior in a computer.

16. The human soul is vastly more complicated than the animals because it is made in the _____ of God.

17. When Steven Weinberg said, "Scientists may have to bypass the problem of human consciousness altogether because it may just be too hard for us," what he meant was it wasn't giving them (evolutionists) the _____ they wanted; therefore they were going to ignore the evidence.

18. There is data proving that your conscious life can actually reconfigure your _____."

19. How can the existence of a soul give us a new way to understand how God can be everywhere? _____

20. God occupies space in the same way the soul occupies the _____.

21. Lee Strobel makes the statement that his ability to ponder, reason, speculate, imagine, and feel emotion proves that his mind could not have been the evolutionary byproduct of brute, mindless _____.

22. Lee Strobel quoted Stuart Hackett as saying, "I think, therefore _____ is."

Chapter 11: Final Exam

1. _____—Darwin believed the cell to be the most complex building blocks of all nature.

2. _____—After performing over 1000 brain surgeries, Dr. Penfield had concrete evidence that the brain and mind are clearly distinct from each other.

3. _____—*Trinity* is the biblical belief that people consist of both body and spirit.

4. _____—When computers which have artificial intelligence reach a certain level of intelligence they will begin to think on their own.

5. _____—The movement of eugenics is "the attempt to improve the human species through the control of hereditary factors in mating."

6. _____—Seth is specifically stated as being Adam and Eve's third son born.

7. _____—The Nebraska Man and his entire family were created from the tooth of an extinct pig.

8. _____—The Cambrian Explosion literally turned Darwin's tree upside-down.

9. _____—Miller's Experiment was proven fraud the same year it was published.

10. _____—True science and faith are at war with each other.

11. _____—Scientific evidence actually supports a theistic belief.

12. _____—Elohim is a word Christians use that means God spoke the universe into existence out of nothing.

13. _____—The fine-tuning of our universe can easily be explained as a cosmic accident.

14. _____—The Bible teaches that the decay and deterioration we see in our world is the result of sin.

15. _____—Science should be the search for truth and not merely the search for materialistic explanations to explain how life came about.

Fill-in-the-Blanks:

1. The DNA of all women on planet earth can be traced back to one woman who geneticists have named _____.

2. The DNA of all men can be traced back to one man who geneticists have named Y-_____.

3. Two different scientists, one an evolutionists and one a creationists, can study the exact same evidence yet derive two totally different conclusions from it because they both begin their work with a preconceived _____.

4. To begin with a specific theory, interpret your data according to that theory, and then claim that your conclusion verifies your theory is called _____.

5. We can limit the age of the earth through observable scientific data by using what's known as the _____.

6. It is impossible for the Colorado River to have formed the Grand Canyon because the river would have had to have flowed _____.

7. The search for the _____ pushed archeology to the forefront in the 1800's.

8. What is the term scientists use when describing a system or machine they find interesting but can't explain? "_____"

9. The cell in Darwin's day looked like nothing more than a little glob of _____.

10. A year-long British study provided evidence that a person's consciousness continues after they are pronounced clinically _____.

11. Our proof that the Bible did not steal from the Koran, but that the Koran stole from the Bible is because Mohammad, the author of the Koran, wasn't even _____ for approximately 500 years after the Bible was completed in its current format.

12. There were two conclusions that could have been reached by studying the evidence Darwin collected from the Galapagos Islands: that all life descended from a common _____, or that all life was the result of a common _____.

Multiple Choice: Choose the very best definition or answer for the following. ...

1. Operational Science is _____.

2. Historical Science is _____.

3. The law of biogenesis states which of the following . . . life never comes from non-life and genetically mutates downhill _____.

4. The most serious theological issue with accepting the theory of evolution *__because it does away with the gospel of Christ__* is . . . _____.

5. Peter prophesied that in the end times scoffers would arise who would *__willfully forget what two historical events__*? . . .

a.

b.

The following multiple choice have more than one answer. Circle all that apply.

1. Consciousness consists of which of the following

   a. Thoughts

b. Emotions

c. Desires

d. Beliefs

e. Free choices

2. Which of the following are *biblical* proofs that Noah's flood was a global historical event?

a. The water remained for over a year.

b. The water was 22 feet over the highest mountain top.

c. Why spend 120 years building an ark when all you had to do was move a few hundred miles away to save your family?

3. Which of the following are *historically* proofs that Noah's flood was a global historical event?

a. 272 stories from all cultures that speak of a global flood

b. The flood account on various archeological tablets that supply the same details as the Bible.

c. Over 100 sightings of Noah's ark on Mt. Ararat dating from the 5th century B.C. to 1990 A.D.

d. The genealogical records of many European kings can be traced back to Japheth, Noah's son.

4. Which of the following are *scientific* proofs that Noah's flood was a global historical event?

a. The existence of the mid-oceanic ridge, continental shelves and slopes.

b. The existence of the Ice Age which could only have occurred as a result of a global flood.

c. The existence of herds of frozen Mammoths and millions of dinosaurs buried alive.

d. The existence of the jigsaw puzzle fit of the continents, indicating they were once all connected.

5. What would be the characteristics of a Cause with the intelligence to create a universe like ours?

a. Finite

b. Beginningless

c. Uncaused

d. Timeless

e. Spaceless

f. Personal

g. Powerful

Short Answer: One or two sentences.

1. How does media bias reveal itself in the Hollywood movie, *Inherit the Wind*?

2. Explain how Exodus 20:8-11 refutes the idea that God created using millions and billions of years?

3. What is the main problem with dating objects or events of *prehistoric* history?

4. What are the two differing views concerning the formation of the Grand Canyon?

5. Define the two types of evolution, microevolution and macroevolution.

6. What is so dangerous about people (Christians or non-Christians) believing Darwin's theory to be actual fact?

7. How did Darwin, his cousin Galton, and Haeckel decide which races were inferior and which were superior?

8. Why are the 17 language families mankind speaks a hindrance to the theory of evolution?

9. In relation to the young earth theory, what are five scientific problems with declaring the earth to be billions of years old? (Look in notes...)

10. How is the fact that man is a conscious being a hindrance to the belief of evolution?

11. What are five serious theological issues with trying to mesh evolution into the biblical story of creation?

a.

b.

c.

d.

e.

f.

g..

h.

i.

12. How did Darwin's theory destroy the lives of Ota Benga and Princess Truganini?

___

Answers for Worksheets, Quizzes and Tests

Chapter 2: What does the Bible Actually Teach?

John 1:1-3 and Colossians 1:15-18—These verses reveal that Jesus is God incarnate, meaning God in the flesh. He is called the Word, and it was through Him that everything created was created. In Colossians 1:15-18 Paul presents Christ as Creator, coeternal with the Father, and over even the highest orders of heaven and earth. John 1:14 further clarifies the fact that Christ is God incarnate by declaring that the Word became flesh and dwelt among men. The Greek word for Word here is Logos, which carries the idea of a unique communication of God to man.

Genesis 1:1—God created man during the first week of creation. Before this "first week of creation there was no such thing as "time" because that was "the beginning."

Psalms 33:6-9—God SPOKE His creation into being. He didn't take a lump of clay like a potter would do to create a finished product, He merely spoke and all that is seen and unseen in the universe came into being—all except man.

Mark 10:3-6—Jesus, creator of all, stated that from the very "beginning of creation" God made them male and female. Who else would know better the method, sequence, and timing of creation than the Creator himself?

Genesis 2:7—God didn't speak man into existence as He did the rest of creation. Instead, He took dust from the ground and formed Adam's body, and then He breathed the breath of life into his nostrils. At the moment God's breath entered Adam's body, man became a living being.

Genesis 1:31—God gives us the exact chronological order of His creation, and man lands on day six. Take note for a later discussion that when God finished the creation of man He declared his work "very good." Since this declaration was made on the actual day of man's creation, there was nothing Adam could have done to earn this decree. God declared him "very good" based on His opinion alone. This helps us to understand that our significance comes from our Creator, not from our performance, our opinion, or even the opinions of others.

Romans 5:12 and 1 Corinthians 15:21-22—Sin entered the world through one man's sin, and death through sin. As a result, all of mankind inherited a sin nature and is destined to experience both physical and spiritual death. Yet God's love for us was so strong that He sent the Second Adam, the Lord Jesus Christ, to pay the wages for our sin on Calvary so that we could be reunited with Him.

2 Peter 3:3-6—Peter prophesized that in the end times scoffers would come, mocking the idea that Christ would return for His own. These mockers would also willfully choose to forget that

the world was created by the spoken word of God, and that the earth was destroyed with water during the flood of Noah's day. Is this what we see today? Absolutely. The theory of evolution is taught instead of the story of creation, and even though there are millions of fossils that give evidence that great flood waters once covered the earth, Noah's flood is often repeated as one of those "cute little Bible myths."

Romans 8:22—When Adam fell, God's entire creation suffered. "All of creation groans and labors with pangs" awaiting the coming of the Savior. Why does even nature await the coming of Christ? Because Christ's redemptive work at Calvary extends even to the sin-cursed cosmos itself, meaning that one day God will restore nature to its pre-fall (Garden of Eden) condition.

Acts 3:20-21—Again, God has appointed a time when all of creation will be restored to its original perfect state of being.

1 Corinthians 15:45-49—Even as the first Adam became a living being, the Last Adam (Christ) became a life-giving Spirit so that all who trust in Him will not be held in bondage to the power of sin. Instead, we will be reunited with God in eternity. And even though we were originally born of the dust of the ground, in eternity we will bear the image of Christ in glorified bodies.

Chapter 3: Why Should Christians Study Evolution?

1. Why is it important for Christians to know the Bible? We have to know it in order to defend why we believe what we believe. Paul said to study to show ourselves approved

2. Give two reasons why it is important for Christians to understand the theory of evolution. We need to know our enemy in order to answer their arguments, and we need to know how to witness to an evolutionist, showing them that what we believe does fit into the reality of our world.

3. Define and explain the two types of science. Operational Science—science that must be observable with one or more of our five senses or experimentally repeatable so that it can be tested and potentially falsifiable. Historical Science—historical science involves interpreting evidence from the past and therefore must being with assumptions. It begins with a bias.

4. Why is it important to understand that evolution fits into the historical realm of science? Because it's taught as "operational science" yet it's based on assumptions from the past. This means the conclusions reached were founded upon the bias of the specific scientist who was examining the evidence, and if his beginning assumption or bias was wrong, then chances are his conclusion will be wrong as well.

5. What type of evolution does the Bible support? Give an example with your answer. Microevolution—small changes within kinds or species. From the original two dogs Noah took aboard the ark came all of the breeds we have today. Dogs turned into dogs; cats into cats; elephants into elephants; etc.

6. What is the difference between laws and theories? Laws—have been proven and can't be broken without outside assistance. Theories—are merely one man's ideas, or hypothesis about something but hasn't been proven.

7. Give two ways the law of biogenesis defies evolution? Life never comes from non-life as evolution teaches. Mutations always go down-hill, meaning a loss of genetic information and not an addition to as evolution demands.

8. Cause and effect implies that a design must have what? Give an example with your answer. Design must have a designed. Example: cake must have a cake baker.

9. Give an example of the probability of evolution being true. A fully functional 747 jet being produced by a tornado going through a junk yard.

10. What type of evolution is required for Darwin's theory of evolution to be true? Macro-evolution

Chapter 4: Creation versus Evolution—Puzzle 1

1. Popularized a theory that paved the way for God to be removed in the minds of many: (Darwin)

2. Science that depends on assumptions concerning the past: (historical science)

3. Abbreviation for the true "witch hunters" of the Scopes Trial: (ACLU)

4. Someone's guess that has not been proven true: (theory)

5. When used with the words *evening* and *morning*, a number or ordinal, it always means a solar day: (Yom)

6. The third son of Adam and Eve's mentioned in scriptures—but not their 3rd child: (Seth)

7. Cave men with slight bone issues who were once thought to be the missing link: (Neanderthals)

8. A deliberate hoax pawned off as proof of evolution for 50 years: (Piltdown Man)

9. In the Old Testament scriptures this word always means a set of solar days: (Yamin)

10. Science that is testable and repeatable and potentially falsifiable: (operational science)

11. A fictitious character in the movie *Inherit the Wind* who was used to make Christians look ignorant: (Reverend Brown)

12. Believed that if they killed their classmates, they would merely be "scattering molecules": (Columbine killers)

13. According to Jewish tradition, Adam and Eve had this many children: (fifty-five)

14. Intakes carbon dioxide and lets out oxygen, which allows earth to support human life: (plants)

15. He and his entire family were reconstructed from a single tooth—that of an extinct pig: (Nebraska Man)

16. God created this on the fourth day of creation: (solar system)

17. Assumed by scientists to be the first woman who ever lived from whom all women descended: (Mitochondrial Eve)

18. Life never comes from nonlife: (Law of Biogenesis)

19. Proven by science to be true: (law)

20. A grossly apelike figure hailed as the missing link because tools were found nearby: (Lucy)

21. False drawings of embryos designed to prove the evolution from one species to another which are today still in text books even though they were proven inaccurate nearly 150 years ago: (Haeckel's Embroys)

22. A tree Darwin designed to picture the order of descent from one species to another that has literally been turned up-side down by the discovery known as the Cambrian Explosion: (Darwin's Tree of Life)

23. An experiment that some evolutionists claim produced organic molecules, thus the possibility of life; yet when performed using the accurate atmospheric chemicals actually produced Cyanide, thus eliminating any possibility of producing life: (Miller Experiment)

24. Evolutionists wrongfully claim this creature to be proof of evolution because they say it is "half-bird and half-reptile": (Archaeopteryx)

25. Instead of proceeding from observation to conclusion, the conclusion interprets the observation and is then used to "prove" the conclusion: (circular reasoning)

Chapter 5: Creation versus Evolution—Puzzle 2

1. Our universe must have had a beginning, and therefore, a (Cause).

2. The everyday functioning and coincidences of our universe is without question a (miracle).

3. Scientific evidence actually supports (theistic) belief.

4. The main issue with accurately predicting (past) events is, "We weren't there."

5. A name of God which is plural in form but singular in nature and is the first biblical reference to the Trinity is (Elohim).

6. God transcends the universe and is therefore above the (laws) of nature.

7. Romans 1:20 tells us that God's eternal power and divine nature can be seen and understood through (nature).

8. In the atheistic viewpoint our universe popped into existence out of (nothing) with absolutely no explanation at all.

9. (Ex Nihilo) is a word the Bible uses that means God spoke the universe into existence out of nothing.

10. The basic structure of the universe is balanced on a (Razor's Edge) for life to exist.

11. Albert Einstein developed his general theory of (relativity) in 1915, which is a theory that doesn't allow for a static universe.

12. Science and faith are not at (war) as so many people like to suggest.

13. The cause of the universe must transcend matter, space, and (time).

14. The theory whose (predictions) most accurately fit the evidence is the most likely true.

15. "There are more than (thirty) separate physical or cosmological parameters that require precise calibrations in order to produce a life-sustaining universe" (Strobel 132).

16. Allan Rex Sandage has been dubbed the "Grand Old Man of (Cosmology)."

17. The fine-tuning of our universe cannot be explained as a cosmic (accident).

18. Many scientists of this modern era have been driven to (faith) by their very work.

19. The Bible teaches that the decay and deterioration we see in our world is the result of (sin).

20. To begin with a specific theory, interpret your data according to that theory, and then claim that your conclusion verifies your theory is called (circular-reasoning).

21. Information in the cell requires an intelligent (Designer).

22. The assumption since ancient Greek time was that the world was (eternal).

23. Creation and evolution are two different (world) views.

24. The (Cambrian Explosion) provides not only a negative case against macroevolution, but a positive argument for the biblical story of creation.

25. The (Kalam) argument states that whatever begins to exist has a cause, the universe began to exist, therefore the universe had a cause.

Chapter 6: Mid-way Opportunity

1. The main issue with accurately predicting past events is, "You weren't there."

2. The Cause of the universe must transcend matter, space, and time.

3. The everyday functioning and coincidences of our universe is without question a miracle.

4. God transcends the universe and is therefore above the laws of nature.

5. Atheists believe that our universe popped into existence out of nothing and without a Cause.

6. Information in the cell requires an intelligent designer.

7. Many scientists of this modern era have been driven to faith by their very work.

8. The Kalam argument states that whatever began to exist has a cause, the universe began to exist, and therefore the universe has a Cause.

9. The Cambrian Explosion provides a negative case for evolution and a positive case for creation.

10. What are five inescapable conclusions we must admit if Darwinism is true?

There is no God.

There is no life after death.

There is no absolute foundation for right or wrong.

There is no ultimate reason for life.

People don't really have a free will.

Short Answer:

1. Who were the true witch hunters of the Scopes Trial? American Civil Liberties Union

2. When *yom* is used in the Old Testament with the words evening or morning, or with a number or ordinal, it always refers to a what? It always refers to a solar day.

3. In the Old Testament scriptures when the word *yamin* is used it is always a reference to a set of solar days. What is the significance of this when compared to Exodus 20:8? The very finger of God wrote that the creation of the world was in six solar days. There's no other way to interpret this verse.

4. The Neanderthal man is generally accepted to be nothing more than what? Man

5. What missing link was the product of a complete fraud; yet was passed off as proof of evolution for more than 50 years? Piltdown Man

6. What is the difference between operational and historical science? Operational science is true "test tube" science; historical science isn't repeatable and testable and is based on the assumptions and biased opinions of the scientist.

7. What missing link was created from the tooth of an extinct pig? Nebraska Man

8. Peter prophesied that in the end time scoffers would arise who would willfully forget what two historical events?

a. God spoke creation into being.

b. The global flood that destroyed the entire earth in Noah's day.

9. What biblical problems does it cause when you make the assumption that Seth was the third son born to Adam and Eve? "Who was Cain afraid of"? and "Where did Cain get his wife"?

10. What two ways does the law of biogenesis defy evolution?

a. Life never comes from nonlife.

b. There is never new or added information in mutations.

11. What would be the characteristics of a Cause with the intelligence to create a universe like ours? A Cause who could create our universe would have to be uncaused, beginningless, timeless, spaceless, immaterial, and a personal being with freedom of will and enormous power.

12. What does *ex nihilo* mean? God created everything out of nothing. He literally spoke the universe into existence.

13. Explain how evolutionists use circular reasoning to "prove" their theory is true? It's when you begin with a theory as fact, interpret your data according to that theory, and then claim that your conclusion verifies your theory.

14. What is wrong with dating an organic object such as a rock and calling your conclusion the *absolute age*? There are no accurate methods of dating objects of the past that aren't based on assumptions, and since assumptions are merely guesses, you can't claim that your conclusion is fact.

15. Explain why planet earth can be called the *privileged planet*. "There are thirty separate physical or cosmological parameters that require precise calibration in order to produce a life-sustaining universe"(Stroble 132).

16. Give three scientific principles that were taught in the scriptures long before man was aware of their truthfulness?

a. (Multiple answers. Check back in topic *Science Taught in God's Word.*)

17. What are five serious theological issues with trying to mesh evolution into the biblical story of creation?

a. (Check back in topic *Serious Theological Issues.*)

Short Essay:

1. Write a paragraph explaining how Hollywood's bias can be seen in the movie *Inherit the Wind*.

2. How would you use the information we've discussed so far to witness to an evolutionist friend?

Chapter 7: The *Limiting Age Factor*

(Example) Too little sediment of all kinds in earth's crust: The time needed to accumulate the entire sedimentary crust on the earth's surface is only 1.25 billion years, far too few for the theory of evolution (Morris 88).

1. Galaxies wind themselves up too fast: If our galaxy was more than a few hundred million years old it would be a featureless disc of stars instead of its present spiral shape (Humphreys 1).

2. Earth's rotation slowing down: The earth is presently spinning at a speed of 1046.6 miles per hour at the equator, but every ten months the scientific community sets the atomic clock back one second because it is slowing down. If the earth is slowing down, that means it used to be going faster. Even 70,000,000 years ago, which is far less than is required for the theory of evolution to be true, the earth would have been spinning too fast to sustain life (Hamilton 1).

3. Moon is moving away from the earth at 2 to 3 inches per year: Since the moon affects our ocean tides, the closer it is to us the greater the force of gravity. Only a few million years ago the moon would have been close enough to cause the tides to drown the entire surface of the earth twice a day. (You can only drown once!)

4. Not enough salt in the sea: The current level of salt in the oceans would have accumulated in less than 42,000,000 years, far less than is required for evolution to be true (Humphreys 2).

5. Continents would have been flattened by erosion: With the current rate of the erosion of the continents, all land would be reduced to sea level in merely 14,000,000 years. If the uplift and erosion on our earth had been continuing for even two or three times that 14,000,000 in the past, all of our sedimentary rock would be gone by now (Morris 88).

6. Not enough mud on the sea floor: Twenty billion tons of dirt and rock are deposited in the oceans each year. This material accumulates as loose sediment on the hard lava-formed rock of the ocean floor. With the average depth of all ocean sediment being less than 400 meters, and allowing for the sediment that is removed by the sliding of the ocean floor beneath the continents (only a few cm/year), all the sediment currently on the ocean floor would have accumulated in less than 12,000,000 years, far less than is necessary for the theory of evolution to be true (Humphreys 2).

7. Comets disintegrate too quickly: "According to evolutionary theory, comets are supposed to be the same age as the solar system, about five billion years. Yet each time a comet orbits close to the sun, it loses so much of its material that it could not survive much longer than about 100,000 years. Many comets have typical ages of less than 10,000 years" (Humphreys 2), which fits perfectly into the biblical story of creation.

8. Earth's magnetic field decays too fast: Life would have been impossible had the earth's magnetic field decayed along its present trend for even 20,000 years (Morris 80).

9. Biological material decays too fast: "DNA experts insist that DNA cannot exist in natural environments longer than 10,000 years, yet intact strands of DNA appear to have been recovered from fossils allegedly much older: Neanderthal bones, insects in amber, and even from dinosaur

fossils. Bacteria allegedly 250,000,000 years old apparently have been revived with no DNA damage. Soft tissue and blood cells from a dinosaur have astonished experts" (Humphreys 3).

10. Underground oil deposits are under too much pressure: Geologists believe that there is 20,000 pounds of oil pressure per square inch beneath our planet's surface. At a pressure this great, our planet's crust should have cracked around <u>10,000 to 15,000 years</u> after it formed.

11. Jupiter, Saturn, Uranus, Neptune, and Pluto are cooling off: If these planets are 4.5 billion years old as evolution teaches, they should have cooled off long ago. Their current temperature fits perfectly into the <u>few thousand years</u> of the creation story (Brown, Walt. 1995).

12. Too few supernova remnants: Supernovas, or violently-exploding stars, cause remnants of gas and dust to expand outward rapidly. In the nearby parts of our galaxy, where we can observe the remnants from the explosions, we find evidence for only about 200 supernovas. This number is consistent with only about <u>7,000 years</u> worth of supernovas (Humphreys 1).

13. Too much helium in minerals: Newly-measured rates of helium loss from zircon crystals show that it has been leaking for approximately <u>6,000 years</u> (Humphreys 3).

14. Too little moon dust: With no rain, wind, or water, the dust that falls on the moon's surface stays right there, that's why much time was spent concocting landing pedestals on the first spacecraft to minimize the distance it would sink into the dust. Yet when it landed, there was only about an inch of dust. This measurement fits perfectly into the creationist timeframe of a <u>few thousand years,</u> but it is far less than the 150 feet that was expected for the theory of evolution to be true (Morris 88).

15. Written history is too short: "According to evolutionists, Stone Age *Homo sapiens* existed for 190,000 years before beginning to make written records about 4,000 to 5,000 years ago. Prehistoric man built magnificent monuments, made beautiful cave paintings, and kept records of lunar phases, why would he wait nearly <u>two thousand centuries</u> before using these same skills to record history" (Humphreys 5)?

16. Too much carbon 14 in deep geologic strata: No carbon 14 atoms should exist in any carbon older than 250,000 years, yet it is impossible to find any natural source of carbon below Ice Age strata that does not contain significant amounts of carbon 14. Recent discoveries give further evidence that the earth is only <u>thousands, not billions</u>, of years old (Humphreys 4).

17. Not enough Stone Age skeletons: Using the evolutionist's scenario, prehistoric man should have buried at least 8,000,000,000 of their dead. Also, if their evolutionary time scale is correct, buried bones should be able to last for much longer than 200,000 years, so many of the supposed 8,000,000,000 skeletons should be just beneath the surface, along with their buried artifacts. Yet only a few thousand have been found. This signifies that the <u>stone age was much shorter than evolutionists think, maybe even a mere few hundred years</u> (Humphreys 4).

18. Many strata are too tightly bent: Strata in many mountainous areas that are thousands of feet deep are bent and folded into hairpin shapes. "The conventional geologic time scale says these formations were deeply buried and solidified for *hundreds of millions of years* before they were bent. Yet the folding occurred without cracking, with radii so small that the entire

formation had to be still wet and unsolidified when the bending occurred. This implies that the folding occurred <u>less than thousands of years</u> after deposition" (Humphreys 3).

19. Fossil radioactivity shortens geologic "ages" to a few years: Radiohalos are fossil evidence of radioactive decay.

20. <u>Squashed radiohalos</u> in the Colorado plateau <u>indicate that that they were deposited within months of one another, not hundreds of millions of years</u> apart as required by the conventional geological time scale (Humphreys 3).

Chapter 8: Creation versus Evolution—Puzzle 3

1. New findings in astronomy suggest that our planet is indeed (special).

2. Everything about the earth, its location, size, composition, structure, and surroundings testify to the "degree to which our planet is exquisitely and precariously" (balanced).

3. To survive humans need (twenty-six) elements and a bacterium of about sixteen.

4. Most galaxies fall into the (elliptical) category.

5. The probability of life inhabiting other planets keeps declining as we learn more about our (universe).

6. What really matters is that earth is (located) in the exact place to allow life to exist.

7. Scientists have discovered that Jupiter actually acts as a (shield) to protect us from too many comet impacts.

8. Our moon contributes in unexpected ways to provide a stable (environment) for our planet.

9. The evidence of design is evident from the far reaches of the (Milky Way) down to the inner core of our planet.

10. In *The Case for a Creator,* Gonzaliz concluded, ". . . the universe was designed for observers living in places where they can make scientific (discoveries)."

11. A (Black Box) is a term scientists use to describe a system or machine they find interesting but can't explain.

12. Darwin stated that if "any complex organ existed which could not possibly have been formed by numerous, successive, slight (modifications), my theory would absolutely break down."

13. Life is based on molecular (machines).

14. The only force known to be able to make irreducibly complex machines is (intelligent) design.

15. Science should be the search for (truth) and not merely the search for materialistic explanations to explain how life came about.

16. One of the many proofs that the Bible is God's authentic word is the many (scientific) statements that were written in it long before our world was aware of their truthfulness.

17. We can limit the age of the earth through observable scientific data by using what's known as the (Limiting-Age-Factor)

18. A (catastrophic) mechanism for the formation of the Grand Canyon seems most likely.

19. In order for the traditional theory for the Grand Canyon's formation to be accurate, the Colorado River would have had to have run (uphill).

20. If you take all 50 different types of dinosaurs known to man when they were at young adult stage, their average size would have been that of a (sheep).

21. An (Ice Age) would have been the natural result of a global flood.

22. (Brontosaurus) is the hero dinosaur of Hollywood and many books, yet he never even existed.

23. Fossil evidence indicates that T-Rex walked in a stooped-over position, probably waddled like a duck, and would have needed dentures had he attacked other large dinosaurs because the roots of his (teeth) were only one inch deep.

24. (Leviathan) is the dinosaur recorded in the book of Job about which God said, ". . . nothing on earth is his equal."

25. (Behemoth) is a dinosaur recorded in the book of Job whose name means "kingly, gigantic beast."

Chapter 9: Quiz over Reading Material

1. According to Darwinists, when the brain reached a certain level of structure and complexity, people became conscious, meaning they suddenly developed subjectivity, feelings, hopes, point-of-view, and self-awareness.

2. In 1871, Thomas Huxley believed that the mind was a function of matter when it attained a certain degree of organization.

3. A computer will never attain consciousness because all it can do is "shuffle symbols."

4. The existence of consciousness in human beings is strong evidence against Darwinism and for a Creator.

5. After performing surgery on more than 1000 epileptic patients, Wilder Penfield encountered concrete evidence that the brain and mind are actually distinct from each other although clearly connected. What was that evidence? Patients were unable to mentally prevent movement in their bodies when their brain was stimulated electrically, indicating a difference between their mind and body.

6. What is dualism? The biblical belief that people consist of both a body and spirit.

7. MIT's Marvin Minsky stated that the brain was merely a "computer made of meat."

8. What did the year-long British study given in the text provide evidence of? The study provided evidence that the consciousness continues after a person's brain has stopped functioning and he or she is declared clinically dead.

9. What was that evidence? About 10% of sixty-three heart attack victims who were declared clinically dead but were later revived and interviewed reported having well-structured, lucid thoughts, with memory formation and reasoning during the time that their brains were not functioning.

10. Consciousness consists of what six entities?

a. sensations

b. thoughts

c. emotions

d. desires

e. beliefs

f. free choices

11. What did Jesus describe the soul and body as being? Separate from each other.

12. What are three logical implications if physicalism is true?

a. Consciousness doesn't really exist.

b. There is really no free will.

c. There is no disembodied intermediate state.

13. "The scientist can know about the brain by studying it, but he can't know about the mind without asking the person to reveal it."

14. Computers have artificial intelligence, not true intelligence.

15. Consciousness is what causes behavior in conscious beings, but electrical circuitry is what causes behavior in a computer.

16. The human soul is vastly more complicated than the animals because it is made in the image of God.

17. When Steven Weinberg said, "Scientists may have to bypass the problem of human consciousness altogether because it may just be too hard for us," what he meant was it wasn't giving them (evolutionists) the answers they wanted; therefore they were going to ignore the evidence.

18. There is data proving that your conscious life can actually reconfigure your brain.

19. How can the existence of a soul give us a new way to understand how God can be everywhere? Our soul occupies our body without being located in any one part of it.

20. God occupies space in the same way the soul occupies the body.

21. Lee Strobel makes the statement that his ability to ponder, reason, speculate, imagine, and feel emotion proves that his mind could not have been the evolutionary byproduct of brute, mindless matter.

22. Lee Strobel quoted Stuart Hackett as saying, "I think, therefore God is."

Final Exam

True/False:

1. False—Darwin believed the cell to be the most complex building blocks of all nature.

2. True—After performing over 1000 brain surgeries, Dr. Penfield had concrete evidence that the brain and mind are clearly distinct from each other.

3. False—*Trinity* is the biblical belief that people consist of both body and spirit.

4. False—When computers which have artificial intelligence reach a certain level of intelligence they will begin to think on their own.

5. True—The movement of eugenics is "the attempt to improve the human species through the control of hereditary factors in mating."

6. False—Seth is specifically stated as being Adam and Eve's third son born.

7. True—The Nebraska Man and his entire family were created from the tooth of an extinct pig.

8. True—The Cambrian Explosion literally turned Darwin's tree upside-down.

9. True—Miller's Experiment was proven fraud the same year it was published.

10. False—True science and faith are at war with each other.

11. True—Scientific evidence actually supports a theistic belief.

12. False—Elohim is a word Christians use that means God spoke the universe into existence out of nothing.

13. False—The fine-tuning of our universe can easily be explained as a cosmic accident.

14. True—The Bible teaches that the decay and deterioration we see in our world is the result of sin.

15. True—Science should be the search for truth and not merely the search for materialistic explanations to explain how life came about.

Fill-in-the-Blanks:

1. The DNA of all women on planet earth can be traced back to one woman who geneticists have named <u>Mitochondrial Eve</u>.

2. The DNA of all men can be traced back to one man who geneticists have named <u>Y-Chromosome Adam</u>.

3. Two different scientists, one an evolutionists and one a creationists, can study the exact same evidence yet derive two totally different conclusions from it because they both begin their work with a preconceived <u>bias</u>.

4. To begin with a specific theory, interpret your data according to that theory, and then claim that your conclusion verifies your theory is called <u>circular reasoning</u>.

5. We can limit the age of the earth through observable scientific data by using what's known as the Limiting Age Factor.

6. It is impossible for the Colorado River to have formed the Grand Canyon because the river would have had to have flowed uphill.

7. The search for the missing link pushed archeology to the forefront in the 1800's.

8. What is the term scientists use when describing a system or machine they find interesting but can't explain? "A Black Box"

9. The cell in Darwin's day looked like nothing more than a little glob of Jello.

10. A year-long British study provided evidence that a person's consciousness continues after they are pronounced clinically dead.

11. Our proof that the Bible did not steal from the Koran, but that the Koran stole from the Bible is because Mohammad, the author of the Koran, wasn't even born for approximately 500 years after the Bible was completed in its current format.

12. There were two conclusions that could have been reached by studying the evidence Darwin collected from the Galapagos Islands: that all life descended from a common ancestor, or that all life was the result of a common Designer.

Multiple Choice: Choose the very best definition or answer for the following. ...

1. Operational Science is . . . the study of science that is testable with one or more of our five senses

2. Historical Science is . . . the study of objects or events from the past that must begin with assumptions.

3. The law of biogenesis states which of the following . . . life never comes from non-life and genetically mutates downhill (loss of information).

4. The most serious theological issue with accepting the theory of evolution ***because it does away with the gospel of Christ*** is . . . it places Adam as the result of millions of years of death instead of the creator of sin.

5. Peter prophesied that in the end times scoffers would arise who would ***willfully forget what two historical events***? . . . that there was once a global flood and that by the very spoken word of God the heavens and earth were created.

The following multiple choice have more than one answer. Circle all that apply.

1. Consciousness consists of which of the following

b Thoughts

d. Emotions

e. Desires

f. Beliefs

i. Free choices

2. Which of the following are *biblical* proofs that Noah's flood was a global historical event?

b. The water remained for over a year.

c. The water was 22 feet over the highest mountain top.

e. Why spend 120 years building an ark when all you had to do was move a few hundred miles away to save your family?

3. Which of the following are *historically* proofs that Noah's flood was a global historical event?

a. 272 stories from all cultures that speak of a global flood

b. The flood account on various archeological tablets that supply the same details as the Bible.

d. Over 100 sightings of Noah's ark on Mt. Ararat dating from the 5th century B.C. to 1990 A.D.

e. The genealogical records of many European kings can be traced back to Japheth, Noah's son.

4. Which of the following are *scientific* proofs that Noah's flood was a global historical event?

a. The existence of the mid-oceanic ridge, continental shelves and slopes.

d. The existence of the Ice Age which could only have occurred as a result of a global flood.

e. The existence of herds of frozen Mammoths and millions of dinosaurs buried alive.

f. The existence of the jigsaw puzzle fit of the continents, indicating they were once all connected.

5. What would be the characteristics of a Cause with the intelligence to create a universe like ours?

a. Finite

b. Beginningless

d. Uncaused

e. Timeless

f. Spaceless

i. Personal

j. Powerful

Short Answer: One or two sentences.

1. How does media bias reveal itself in the Hollywood movie, *Inherit the Wind*? Details are switched making the Christians look like fools and the evolutionists look highly education and of superior intelligence.

2. Explain how Exodus 20:8-11 refutes the idea that God created using millions and billions of years? The Hebrew word for days is Yamin and it always, without exception, means a set of solar days. Yamin is used in these verses to describe the six days of creation. Also, when the Hebrew word for day, Yom, is used with a number, ordinal, or the words "evening" or "morning", it always means a solar day.

3. What is the main problem with dating objects or events of *prehistoric* history? You must begin with assumptions because you weren't there.

4. What are the two differing views concerning the formation of the Grand Canyon? A small amount of water over a huge amount of time formed the canyon; or a huge amount of water over a small amount of time formed it.

5. Define the two types of evolution, microevolution and macroevolution. Microevolution—small changes within a kind or species; macroevolution—one kind or species changing into another kind or species (cat into horse)

6. What is so dangerous about people (Christians or non-Christians) believing Darwin's theory to be actual fact? The theory does away with the gospel of Christ because it discredits sin as being the cause of death, but teaches that death was the cause of the evolution of man. Therefore, if one man didn't bring sin into the world, the neither can One Man take sin away.

7. How did Darwin, his cousin Galton, and Haeckel decide which races were inferior and which were superior? Using physical features—color of skin, size and shape of noses, etc.

8. Why are the 17 language families mankind speaks a hindrance to the theory of evolution? They all appeared around the same time historically, and they have no evolution from one to another. In other words, there is no connection between the languages so where did they all appear from?

9. In relation to the young earth theory, what are five scientific problems with declaring the earth to be billions of years old? (Look in notes…)

10. How is the fact that man is a conscious being a hindrance to the belief of evolution? They have no way to explain why how man became a conscious being. They can only try to explain where our physical bodies came from.

11. What are five serious theological issues with trying to mesh evolution into the biblical story of creation?

a. Evolution places Adam as the product of millions of years of death instead of its originator.

b. Man breathes in oxygen, plants take in carbon dioxide. This means that plants and humans (animals included) must coexist in the environment in order for either to survive.

c. In Genesis 2:7 God says that Adam was made from the dust of the ground. An ape and dust are two very different things.

d. Where did Eve come from?

e. At the end of the sixth day of creation God pronounced His creation *very good.* Yet if Adam was the product of millions of years of death, disease, violence, parasites, fungi, and bloodshed, which is what evolution teaches, and God called this *very good,* then what kind of a God do we serve?

f. Note that Adam lived through the sixth and seventh days of creation before falling to temptation.

g. Note that the sequence of events in the theory of evolution and the creation story are different.

h. Jesus, who is given the credit for the creation of all, stated that "from the *beginning* He created them male and female."

i. Finally, if the days of creation were really millions of years instead of solar days, then God isn't a very good writer because of the words He used.

12. How did Darwin's theory destroy the lives of Ota Benga and Princess Truganini? Both were treated as museum exhibits and the missing link.

Final Assignment: Write a five page paper over the following topic: What I have learned in this course and how I plan to incorporate that knowledge into my classroom instruction to help build my students' understanding of how science is helping to validate the truthfulness of the biblical account of creation as found in Genesis.

Completion Form for Creation Versus Evolution: A Biblical and Scientific Study (ACSI Registration Number 2,177)

Please print off and initial each of the below assignments verifying you have completed the required work while taking this course. (If you're unable to print the Completion Form, a retyped version will be fine.

_____--I have read all the material assigned in this creation course.
_____--I have completed all chapters, including quizzes and tests, assigned in this creation course.
_____--I have checked the answers to the quizzes, tests and worksheets assigned in the course with their answer keys.
_____--I have completed reading *The Case for a Creator* by Lee Strobel.
_____--I have completed reading *Evolution's Fatal Fruit* by Tom DeRosa.
_____--I have enclosed a copy of my 5 page paper as my final assignment required to receive my 5 CEU's in biblical education.
_____--I have watched 6 hours from the suggested videos over the topic of Creation Versus Evolution. (You can substitute two hours of the suggested videos with other creation videos of your choice if you are unable to purchase or rent the suggested videos.)

Teacher's Name: _____

(Please print name below)
_____

School: _____

Address: _____

Date of Completion: _____

When completed mail form to:

Rockie Fordham
P.O. Box 595
Fountain, Colorado 80817

Additional books to read to assist in reaching your children and those around you for Christ

Jake and the Heavenly Host by RockieSue Fordham (www.rocklanpublications.com). This is a youth (ages 10 to 14) fiction mystery with the gospel presented in it. It contains drama, suspense, mystery, terrorists and spiritual warfare. Your teen will have difficulty putting it down! Available through RockLan Publications, Amazon Books or Kindle e-books—also Amazon Books.

Hidden in My Heart by Wilma Daffern available through www.hiddeninmyheart.info or by e-book (Kindle) through Amazon Books.

Additional Books to Read Over Creation Versus Evolution Topic

Evolution's Fatal Fruit by Tom DeRosa
The Case for Christ by Lee Strobel
The Young Earth Theory by John D. Morris
Refuting Evolution by Jonathan Sarfait Ph.D.
Refuting Evolution 2 by Jonathan Sarfait Ph.D
Grand Canyon: a different view by Tom Vail
Noah's Ark and the Lost World by Dr. John D. Morris (Children's book but I loved it too)
The Great Dinosaur Mystery and the Bible by Paul S. Taylor (Children's book but great)
The Exodus Case (New Discoveries Confirm the Historical Exodus) by Dr. Lennart Moller
Evolution Exposed by Roger Patterson

References

(Books)

Cavalli-Sfora, L.L., *Genes, Peoples and Languages,* Penguin Books, London, 2001.

Combee—Jerry H. Combee, Ph.D., *The History of the Word in Christian Perspective,* (Pensacola, Florida: A Beka Book Publications, 1979)

Corbin—B. J. Corbin, *The Explorers of Ararat: and the Search for Noah's Ark,* (Long Beach, California: Great Commission Illustrated Books, 1999)

Darwin—Charles Darwin, *The Autobiography of Charles Darwin,* (New York, NY: W.W. Norton & Company, Inc., 1969)

DeRosa—Tom DeRosa, *Evolution's Fatal Fruit,* (Fort Lauderdale, Florida: Coral Ridge Ministries, 2006)

Faith Quest, Vol. 2: Student Edition, (Nashville, Tennessee: LifeWay Christian School Resources, 178-179)

Hoyle, Fred & Wickramasignhe, N.C.: "The Intelligent Universe", page 527. (Rubix cube analogy)

Menton—Dr. David N. Menton, *Inherit the Wind: A Hollywood History of the Scopes Trial,* (Hebron,

Kentucky: Answers in Genesis, 2006)

Moller—Lennart Moller, *The Exodus Case,* (Copenhagen NV, Denmark: Scandinavia Publishing House, 2002)

Morris—John D. Morris, Ph.D., *The Young Earth,* (Green Forest, Arkansas: Master Books, 1994)

Morris—John D. Morris, *Noah's Ark and the Lost World,* (El Cajon, California: Master Books, 1990)

Patterson—Roger Patterson, *Evolution Exposed Biology,* (Hebron, Kentucky: Thomas Nelson, Inc., 2007)

Sarfati—Jonathan D. Sarfati, PH.D., F.M., *Refuting Evolution,* (Green Forest, AR: Master Books, Inc., 1999)

Schmeikart & Allen—*A Patriot's History of the Chaptered States*, (New York, New York: Penguin Group, 2004)

Strobel—Lee Strobel, *The Case for Christ,* (Grand Rapids, Michigan: Zondervan Publishing House, 1998)

Strobel—Lee Stroble, *The Case for a Creator,* (Grand Rapids, Michigan: Zondervan Publishing House, 2004)

Taylor—Paul S. Taylor, *The Great Dinosaur Mystery and the Bible,* (Colorado Springs, Colorado: Cook Communications Ministries, 1989)

Vail—Tom Vail, *Grand Canyon, a Different View,* (Green Forest, Arkansas: Master Books, 2003)

(Articles)

Bates, Gary: "An Awesome Mind", *Creation, 26(3)* June-Aug. 2004, AIG, pg. 36-41

Ham, Ken: "Public Schools—some sad statistics", *Answers Update,* AIG, (Excerpted from the 18 August broadcast of Answers . . . with Ken Ham) www.answersingenesis.org/radiolog

Williams, Alexander (B.Sc.): "Language Problems for Evolutionists", AIG

Ham, Ken: "Lincoln and Darwin", Answers update 16:2; AIG (Excerpted from February 12, 2009 broadcast of the Answers . . . with Ken Ham, www.answersingenesis.org/radiolog

Answers in Genesis Ministries, www.answersingenesis.org/chimps

Morris, Dr. Henry M.: "Evolutionary Arrogance", *Acts and Facts*, July 2009, page 8

Manne, Robert: "A Stolen Generation" May 2, 2005

Ham, Ken: "Darwin's Plantation", *One Blood*, January 8, 2009

Lansdown, Anders: *Creation* 15(1), 26-29, AIG; December 1992

Austin, Steven: "Grand Canyon: Monument to Catastrophe", 94

Hamilton, Donald L.: www.pages.prodigy.com/suna/earth.htm

Humphreys, Dr. Russell: "Evidence for a Young World", *Impact* #384, ICR; June 2005

Morris, John D.: "The Young Earth" (Arkansas: Master Books, Inc., 1994)

Walt Brown, "In the Beginning: Compelling evidence for creation and the flood" (1995)

www.creationwiki.org/Jupiter_and_Saturn_are_cooling_too_rapidly_to_be_old

www.answersingenesis.org/docs/4005.asp?vPrint=1.

Made in the USA
Lexington, KY
01 March 2014